BEHIND THE BUZZER

THE MASK CRACKED, SHE DIDN'T.

BY
NICOLA HARPER

BEHIND THE BUZZER: THE MASK CRACKED, SHE DIDN'T.

Author: Nicola Harper

Copyright © 2025 Nicola Harper

The author asserts the moral right to be identified as the author of this work.

The right of Nicola Harper to be identified as author of this work has been asserted by the author in accordance with section 77 and 78 of the Copyright, Designs and Patents Act 1988.

First Published in 2025

ISBN 978-1-83538-625-5 (Paperback)
    978-1-83538-626-2 (Hardback)
    978-1-83538-627-9 (E-Book)

Book Cover Design by: Nicola Harper

Book Layout by:
  White Magic Studios
  www.whitemagicstudios.co.uk

Published by:
  Maple Publishers
  Fairbourne Drive, Atterbury,
  Milton Keynes,
  MK10 9RG, UK
  www.maplepublishers.com

A CIP catalogue record for this title is available from the British Library.

All rights reserved. No part of this book may be reproduced or translated in any form or by any means, electronic or mechanical, including photocopying, recording or by any information storage and retrieval system without written permission from the author.

The views expressed in this work are solely those of the author and do not reflect the opinions of Publishers, and the Publisher hereby disclaims any responsibility for them. This book should not be used as a substitute for the advice of a competent authority, admitted or authorized to advise on the subjects covered.

Contents

	Prologue	4
Chapter One	Maiden Experience	7
Chapter Two	The Girl	15
Chapter Three	Testing the Waters & Finding my Feet	34
Chapter Four	Perverse Men & Willing Addicts	51
Chapter Five	A Jamaican Farewell	62
Chapter Six	Tricks and Treats	68
Chapter Seven	Old is Gold	79
Chapter Eight	Unique Encounter	86
Chapter Nine	Luke, The Gift Horse	100
Chapter Ten	Fetishes & Peccadilloes at The Pelican	110
Chapter Eleven	Surprise Customer	124
Chapter Twelve	'Fuck a Book'	132
Chapter Thirteen	Bizarre Customers	143
Chapter Fourteen	The Stereotypical Brothel: BJ's	152
Chapter Fifteen	Role Play	169
Chapter Sixteen	More Quirky People	175
Chapter Seventeen	Nicola, The Entrepreneur	188
Chapter Eighteen	End.... not yet. What next? Just the Start	210

Prologue

March 2021

Patient No. P09482731 sat on a thin bed in a small single room with four white walls; a sink built into one wall, having buttons instead of taps. A black mesh covered the lone window, blocking a free view of the outside world.

Alarms went off all through the day and night and people in other rooms were screaming like they were being tortured. Loads of nurses shouted to each other when an alarm went and then ran as a group to go and see whoever was screaming. Nine times out of ten, a patient had slit his wrists or, occasionally, his throat. After the nurses entered the person's room, they pinned the screamer to the floor and injected something into him to sedate him. It was crazy to listen to, because one minute the patient was screaming his head off like he was being killed, and the next minute – when the sedation kicked in – everything went quiet. But the guy above her room would be very noisy anyway; constant bangs came through the ceiling as he marched up and down in his room. It was never silent in there…

It smelt of cold air there, because she constantly left the vents in the window grills open. The feel of fresh air gave her a slight sense of normality and took the edge off the feeling that she was trapped in a psychiatric hospital. And it was better than the stench of the long, dark corridor outside, which stank of hospital cleaning products and stale piss.

❄︎❄︎❄︎

Patient No. P09482731 at the Salford psychiatric hospital, that's me, Nicola Harper. I have been sectioned, because I took an overdose trying to end my life after being gaslighted and abused by my husband. I have lost everything. My daughter, my dog, my house, and literally everything that I own. Oh, and also, I'm currently on bail for guns and grenades charges.

My psychiatrist told me that I had been gaslighted by my husband and mine was one of the worst cases of gaslighting he had come across in his entire career. He also told me that I have been given a diagnosis of post-traumatic stress disorder (PTSD). And that mine was a case that was too complicated for him, needing referral to a more senior professional. Hmm.... my psychologist himself says he can't help me; I guess nobody can then? Maybe I'm going properly nuts?

What actually is gaslighting?
What have I got left to live for?
Will I ever be me again?
Will I ever get out of this hospital?
Will these thoughts that are going round in my head ever leave?

My head spins with the cacophony of my thoughts; of my surroundings, of all the abuse I underwent with my husband, and of the thought whether I want to live at all anymore. At this moment in time, I'm not sure if I'll ever get out of this psychiatric hospital. Some people in here have been here for years! It's a strange fact, but at this moment in time, all I have to my name are my thoughts, and I don't want to let them get the better of me. I *can't*.

Over the last few days I realised that, in here, I had to do something, *anything*, to take my mind off my current reality. That may be the only way I could retain my sanity; at least, whatever is left of it. They had offered me paper, pencil and crayons to distract me. I grabbed them and went to work. I found that the process of writing – and looking back on the life that I had lived – helped to take my mind off everything else, including the screaming in the corridor. These scraps of paper with my writing slowly morphed into a book; a book about my life...

I've been writing this book every day. I make notes about what I've done with my life and this really does help to keep the negative thoughts away. Thank God! Writing my life story is literally saving my life!

If just one woman reads this book, and it somehow stops her from having to go through the abuse that I've been through, then it will have served its purpose, and I'll be happy. I don't know what's going to happen to me, but at least my story will be out in the world, and will live forever. It may even help to change a few lives for the better...

Chapter One
Maiden Experience

Every prostitute remembers their first customer like it was yesterday and I am certainly no exception. I can vividly visualize walking into a bedroom at *The Edwardian* for the very first time and seeing Jonathan there as he stood there completely naked. He had a right fuzzy, hairy body and he was quite chubby but not fat. His penis was average in size and it was already semi-hard. He was holding a small glass bottle in his hand.

I couldn't believe this man had picked me – out of all the other girls - considering how I was dressed. When I'd got the call from the brothel receptionist to say they would give me a working interview – where you basically go in and work the shift – I'd felt so stressed, mainly because I didn't know what to wear. I'd presumed that prostitutes had to dress like the street girls you see in movies and on TV, that the dirtier and sluttier they looked, the better. So I'd quickly gone round the charity shops and bought bright red lipstick, hideous heels I couldn't stand up in, fishnet stockings, a short skirt, a Basque and a pair of tacky bright red crotchless knickers. I'd backcombed my blonde hair and put my make up on really heavy like they do in films.

At that point, I'd never been inside a brothel before, and I had visions of *The Edwardian* – a massage parlour in Manchester - being all filthy and seedy, like a stereotypical one that's shown in the media. To be honest, I was expecting a dirty building packed with gross rooms that were full of piss-stained mattresses and portable TVs with coat hangers for aerials that played cheesy porn from old video machines. But I was about to learn how wrong I was, and how different brothels actually are compared with what Joe Public thinks.

At ten o'clock, when it was time for my shift to start, I parked my car at the back of the huge, white building, and walked round to the front door. It was a dark September night, and I remember pulling my coat tightly round me, trying to keep the cold away. I'd just bought it from the charity shop opposite my new house, but when I'd taken it home I'd found that the bloody thing was full of fleas, so I had to go out and nick some flea spray from Boots as I had no money left. Anyway, I saw that there was an intercom system with buttons next to the door, similar to those that you get in flats. I pressed a button, a buzzer went off, the door clicked open, and I walked in. And got the shock of my life.

This place was not what I'd been expecting at all. It was spotlessly clean and I reckoned that thousands of pounds had been spent on doing it up. The walls looked freshly painted and there were colourful, arty pictures everywhere. The carpets and soft furnishings had neutral tones and it all looked very tasteful. Later, I would discover that there were seven bedrooms in *The Edwardian*, all decorated with different themes, like the

Penthouse, the Gold room, the Blue room and the Fantasy room. Each one of them was stylishly done up, with expensive showers, beds and carpets. There was nothing seedy about this place at all.

The receptionist, Tracy, introduced herself and then showed me into the backroom. As she opened the door, I saw three totally stunning girls standing there. I was gobsmacked, because they looked nothing like the street girls I'd been expecting. First, there was Gypsy. She was beautiful and only a couple of years older than me at twenty nine. She had long, silky, jet black hair, big dark eyes, and was tanned from head to toe. She was a slim size ten, with big, natural 34D boobs. She was dressed in a black satin bra, with matching knickers. Next to Gypsy was Cindy.

She was also very pretty and she looked young, maybe about eighteen. She had long, blonde hair, huge blue eyes and an English rose complexion. She was tiny, probably a dress size six, with small 32B boobs. She was dressed in skimpy red underwear. Last, but not the least, was a gorgeous, glamorous girl called Olivia. She also had long blonde hair and big, blue eyes. She was very tanned and probably a petite dress size eight, with small 32B boobs. She was dressed in the most dazzling, gleaming white satin Basque.

Wow, I thought. *I look hideous compared to these three, with my back combed hair, my punk rocker make up and my mismatched street walking outfit. Not to mention my crotchless knickers. How wrong was I, thinking the way I did about these women?*

All the girls turned to look at me as I entered the room. They had shock on their faces, probably because I looked like an absolute cunt compared to them. All three of them looked glamorous and sexy, whereas I looked like a dirty street whore. *I'm not going to make any money with these three with me*, I thought to myself. *Who is going to pick me over them?* I was a size ten to twelve back then with no boobs, a fat sloppy ass and loads of stretch marks. I felt like absolute shit as I stood next to these three stunners.

Suddenly, there was a buzzing noise coming from the intercom in the room.

"Can you come through, girls?" A voice shouted.

Gypsy looked at me.

"We all have to go and say hello to a customer," she said.

"Okay," I replied. I followed the other three ladies into the reception area.

There was a man seated on the leather Chesterfield in the reception room, dressed quite smartly in a pink shirt and blue, office-type trousers. He was quite stocky, tall, with a huge bald head and red cheeks.

The other three walked in front of him.

"Hi, Jonathan," they all said, before turning and walking back to the girls' room.

I didn't know what to do, so I just stood there.

"Hello," I said, my voice sounding sheepish. I felt like a spare part. Jonathan looked at me.

"What's your name?" He asked. His voice was very feminine, almost camp.

"Nicola," I said. "I mean Nicole," I corrected myself quickly. I'd already decided that I wasn't going to use my real name while I was there. Jonathan asked me if I specialised in anything.

"What do you mean?" I said, feeling confused.

"A-levels and O-levels, Nicole," Tracy called from her desk.

"Oh," I said, surprised. I hadn't realised we needed qualifications to do this job. *It must be because this is an upmarket establishment*, I thought to myself. *Maybe they only employ educated women.* "Well," I said. "I've got ten GCSE's, all A's, B's and C's. They didn't do O-levels when I was at school. I didn't do my A-levels because I got pregnant at sixteen."

There was a pause, while Tracy and Jonathan both looked at me with shock on their faces. Then they burst out laughing.

"You really haven't done this before, have you?" Tracy said, smiling at me. She explained that in a brothel, different girls specialise in different things. A-levels stands for anal sex, and O-levels means oral sex without the guy wearing a condom.

"Oh," I said. "I don't mind sucking a guy without a condom, but I'm not doing anal as I've never done it before." I then explained to them that I didn't know how to put a condom on, as I'd only ever had one long-term partner and we'd never used one.

"I'll take her," Jonathan said to Tracy, meaning me. Tracy nodded.

"Nicole," she said. "Can you take Jonathan up to room three, and then come back down to me?" I nodded, and did as she'd asked. I left Jonathan in the room upstairs, then walked back down to reception. I couldn't believe that this man had picked me over the other three girls, looking the way I did. I was made up.

"Right," Tracy said, when I'd reached her desk. "You couldn't have asked for a better first customer. Jonathan doesn't have full sex and he loves being the first to go with our new ladies. He usually has only a blow job. He's booked you for half an hour, so go upstairs and do him, and when you've finished make sure your room is tidy. Then come back downstairs. Okay?"

"No problem," I replied.

So that is how I came to be walking in to room three at *The Edwardian*, to see my very first customer, Jonathan.

"Come here and give me a big hug, Nicole," he said, as I closed the door behind me. "Don't worry, I'm like a big teddy bear. I'm clean, not like some of the dirty cunts you get in here."

"What do I have to do?" I said, walking towards him. A strong scent of Joop aftershave whooshed up my nose as I approached. My voice was quiet.

"Just kneel in front of me and suck my dick slowly so I get loads of pre-cum oozing out of it," he said.

"What's in that bottle?" I asked, pointing at the small glass thing he was clenching it tightly in his right hand.

"Its poppers," Jonathan said. "I sniff it while I'm coming because it makes it more intense when I explode. Do you want to try some?"

"No thanks," I said.

I watched as Jonathan walked over to the corner of the room, and stood against the wall. He closed his eyes and started to sniff his poppers. I walked over, knelt on the floor in front of him, and started to slowly lick the end of his stiff prick. It tasted and smelt of soap.

"Oh Nicole, that is so good," he said, his voice a delighted squeak. "Go slower."

So I went as slowly as I could, licking up and down the sides of his cock, then sucking the end nice and slow, letting all the pre-cum ooze out of the end of his stiff prick, until eventually he exploded in my mouth.

"Wowee Nicole," Jonathan said, opening his eyes. "That was fantastic."

"Thanks," I said.

As I watched him go and get into the shower, I realised that I was now officially a prostitute. I had had sex with a man for money. There was no going back.

I walked back down to the girls' room feeling great. A year ago, I would never have thought I would be working in a brothel twelve months on. But actually, compared with the years of domestic violence I'd just experienced at the hands of my long-term partner Matt, sucking off Jonathan - and being with the other girls at *The Edwardian* - felt surprisingly good. Jonathan had complimented me, and I'd been in charge of making him feel ecstatic. It was a kind of power, to cause that sort of intense feeling in another human being. And the brothel felt like a safe, classy place to work in. I liked it there.

As the buzzer went off again and we were all called into the reception area to say hello to another client, I couldn't have predicted that I was just starting out on what would be a crazy, roller-coaster ride of a lifetime, one that would lead me to places, customers and sex fetishes that I never thought existed…

Chapter Two
The Girl

I was born and bred in a two bedroom terraced house in Stretford, Manchester. It's red-bricked with a white front door, and my Mum still lives there today. She was a single parent and she did her very best with me, and to be honest I never wanted for anything. She always gave me, within her power, everything that she could, and I'll forever be grateful to her for that. I did see my Dad on some weekends, but my main memories of growing up are of being with Mum. Because it was just the two of us, we used to go everywhere together; shopping, seeing friends, to the salons and cafes. I can remember one time when it was raining, we were holding hands and singing and dancing round the street together, not caring that we were getting soaked. We were – and are - extremely close, and nothing will ever change that.

I always associate the aroma of fresh washing that has just been dried on the line with my Mum's house. I love that smell. Another sensory memory is that every Sunday, the smell of a delicious roast would fill her house. It still does to this day. My Mum's favourite scent is Chanelle Mademoiselle perfume, and it wafts past you whenever she walks past. Whenever I smell it on someone else when I'm not with her, it always reminds me of her straight away.

I loved my Nana – my Mum's mother - very much too and I can remember one time when she took me and my cousin Gina for a holiday at Pontins; we all had the best time there. We were either on the beach or at the funfair every day for a week, eating candyfloss and seeing how many times we could go on the Waltzer without feeling sick. Those are some of my really happy childhood memories.

❈❈❈

As I grew older, my rebellious nature became more obvious, and I started getting in trouble a lot at secondary school. I can remember the smells there – particularly the distinctive ones of apple pie and flapjacks in the canteen. In terms of sound memories, it was just full of screaming children. To be fair, I was probably one of the loudest; I never shut up, and I still don't now, to be honest! It was a strict Catholic place, and all the rules there didn't sit well with me. Even though I was spoiled rotten at home, I started acting up in the classroom. I became quite naughty and I can remember one time when I stood on a table and jumped out of a window with a computer (which I then sold as I needed money for weed). There was no good reason for this, maybe I just wanted attention? Who knows.

By the time I was thirteen I was sniffing deodorant, taking speed and smoking weed. I was always hanging around the streets with my friends; the good thing was that we all lived close to each other in Stretford – and some were from nearby Old Trafford. We had a lot of fun together in those days, although my Mum went nuts whenever I got in trouble at school. Graham was also part of the gang I was with then, and he features in a big way later on in my writing.

We would hang around Old Trafford – a rough part of Manchester – taking gas and smoking. Sometimes we would break into factories and I can remember one time when we robbed a cake factory on Ayres Road. We'd all decided to climb over the fence there one pitch-black night, and somehow we got into the building. I can still remember the sweet, sugary smell that filled every room in there. A few minutes later, we all came running out with dozens of boxes of cakes.

But I didn't have time to hang around for long, I had to go back to my Mum's – just like all the other kids had to return to their parents places – however the only problem was that I was now carrying loads of cakes. So I had gone back to my Mum's thinking how fantastic it was that I had these doughnuts and freshly baked muffins and cookies, but obviously I couldn't tell her that I'd just robbed a factory. So I told her I'd found them in a bin. But quite rightly, because I'd said I'd got them out of the trash, she put them all straight into our bin! Looking back, I think I was just a horrible kid - there was no real reason for me to behave the way I did - I was just a rebellious nightmare.

I stole things because I wanted money for weed, like that computer I jumped out of the window with at school. I used to rob other children's designer coats from the cloakroom and sell them, so that I could go and buy drugs. I'd steal clothes from shops and go and buy weed, although when I took them back to my Mum's to store for a while I'd lie and say that someone sold them to me. When my Mum gave me money to go and buy clothes from nice shops, I'd go and get cheap tops and trousers from the market – and tell her they were from Top Shop – then I'd go and spend the rest on drugs. I was really bad back then.

I wasn't addicted to weed or anything – I did it because you were the 'in' one if you had a lot of it. We'd all do it, and we'd go and sit in this guy's house to smoke it. I remember how we used to give each other blowbacks when we were upside down doing handstands. You're just daft when you're a kid. You're experimental, rebellious. I certainly was, anyway.

Pregnancy

I got pregnant when I was sixteen, and that put an end to my crazy lifestyle. For a few years, at least. It was my saving grace, because when I left that group they all progressed from softer drugs to heroin. It became normal for them to walk down the street with rolls of foil stuck behind their ears. When I walk past anyone from that group now, I see straight away what those harder drugs have done to them; they've got no teeth in their heads and are always doing things like robbing packs of bacon from shops. But because I had my son, I was never allowed to go back and hang around with them. If I hadn't had him, I'm pretty certain I would have ended up on smack too, because all of that group were doing it. The older lot got the younger lot on it by using peer pressure. There was no hope for any of them. And then their crimes escalated because they needed to find ways to fund their new habit. Some of them are still shoplifters now, all these years on. They've got no life; their heroin habit totally controls them. Being honest, I'm not friends with any of them now, although I do see them out and about in Stretford from time to time. I don't like hanging around with smack-heads, it's not the sort of company I'd choose to be in. Heroin takes peoples' souls away; all their emotion dies.

Graham was the youngest out of that group, and he was the one that everyone picked on because he had holes in his shoes and things like that. He'd had a rough life; people treating him like shit would eventually cause a big change in his thoughts and behaviour. Graham was the one who I bullied into walking with me to some flats in Moss Side, which were in a really rough area – lots of them had no windows in - to go and get some weed off Ken on the eighth floor.

I made Graham come with me because nobody else would; they were too scared. But as Graham was younger than me it was easy to make him do what I said; I was used to being in control with him – a situation that unfortunately changed dramatically as we will find out later on.

Graham got locked up at fifteen and when he got out he vowed that he would never get bullied again. He was done with being other people's punching bag, finished with being told what to do and with being treated like crap by those around him. After he'd done his sentence, he had the attitude of 'I'm not going to let anyone tell me what to do again'.

It was to do with the bullying as well as his prison time; he'd come out with an "I don't give a fuck" attitude, "I don't give a shit what anyone says". He didn't want to be in the control of others any more, he wanted power and to be his own man. I was told that one day somebody gave him a gun, and he immediately realised the power that a gun gave him. That's what changed him. And that's what ended up changing my life too - many years later.

I was in a relationship with my son Scot's father for a bit, but it didn't last because we were so young. There was no way either of us were ready to end our socialising and become boring stay-at-home parents – we were still teenagers for Christ's sake. I ended up getting expelled from school while I was pregnant, after throwing someone else's GCSE art piece at the head master. I can still remember the look on his face as the mixed-media depiction of Marilyn Monroe ricocheted off his forehead. But although I'd been excluded, I had a home tutor for a while. I, then, went back and took my exams and gained all A's, B's and C's. I left education after that and never went back, because I had my son to think about. I remember the day I had him so clearly, and my Mum was there at his birth. He was such a beautiful child. But I was a baby with a baby; I wasn't ready to be tied down at home with a kid full-time, so my Mum ended up looking after Scot a lot so that I could go and hang out with my friends.

BEHIND THE BUZZER

Matt, Bliss and the Calm Before the Storm

I met Matt – my next long-term partner and soon to be husband – in 1998. Even though my son's Dad spoilt me and even brought me a car for my eighteenth birthday, I ended up leaving him for a man who had nothing except a bus pass. This all happened very quickly, and looking back it felt like a whirlwind. In a matter of weeks after meeting Matt for the first time, we were in a relationship and I'd broken up with my son's father. Matt was a DJ in Manchester and was part of the new group I was hanging out with – a different gang of people to those I broke into factories with. He had a strong, hard core Scouse accent, which he seemed to accentuate as he wasn't originally from Liverpool.

It was like – in his head - he'd had to emphasise it in order to fit in. He smelt of Lynx deodorant – the African one – and also of very strong cannabis. Matt was mixed-race and he got bullied because of it, and when we got together even my own Dad was racist towards him; he couldn't stand the man because of his skin colour. A lot of the older generation around where I lived were like that back then.

I thought it was fantastic how Matt and his friends were all DJ-ing and MC-ing, it seemed so exciting especially as I'd been stuck at home for a few years raising my son Scot, while most of my other friends had been out partying since the age of sixteen. I was drawn into this clubbing lifestyle quickly and it was one that I'd never been part of before. I loved going into the clubs with Matt and standing by the decks with him; I felt so proud that he was my boyfriend. Once I'd started partying I got a taste for it, and I didn't stop. I couldn't, it was all too addictive.

The records that Matt and his mates played were RnB and HipHop, and I can remember how my mates and I regularly danced the night away to their beats in front of the DJ booth. I can recall what it felt like to walk into those clubs as clearly as if I'd gone to one yesterday; the smell of the dry ice, the banging sound systems, the strobe lights dividing up the darkness, the mass of people dancing. It was total sensory overload and I couldn't get enough of it. I'd started taking a lot of whiz again with my clubbing friends; I'd become quite big when I'd had my son Scott, but when I did speed I noticed the weight dropping off which felt really good.

All the dancing probably helped to shift it too. After a little while I got so slim that I was able to wear clothes that I'd never been able to before and I started getting loads of attention from men. I dyed my hair blonde and started wearing false tan; it was like I was morphing into a different person and my self-esteem just kept going up and up.

Being with a new man felt really exciting, especially after being with my son's father for so long. Soon, I was completely smitten; it didn't take long for me to fall head-over-heels in love with Matt. It was so nice to be with someone sexually different as well – and he was fantastic in bed. And I felt all this even though - from the outset - there were signs there that Matt could be violent. I'd heard on the grapevine that he'd beaten his ex-girlfriend up, but at the time I was convinced that she was just saying that to everyone because she was jealous that Matt had got with me. I told myself that there was no truth to her words, and that she was just badmouthing him out of spite. But looking back now, especially after everything abusive that he did to me, I can see that she was telling the truth.

To start with, Matt and I lived together in Manchester for a bit. We stayed there for less than a year, then we moved to Wales to live with his Mum. We had a lot of good times together initially; as well as going to the clubs, I used to love it when Matt and I stayed in to smoke weed and listen to music. Life literally felt like one big party at that point, and after being a stay-at-home mother for several years, I was relishing every second of it. For a while, everything was pure fun.

The Abusive Marriage

Matt and I got married. We didn't tell anybody, we just went to the Stockport registrar and got two witnesses off the street to come in with us, and then spent that night in the hotel at the back of the office. Although we didn't go on a honeymoon or anything, it all felt great to me. As far as I was concerned, I was with an amazing man who I loved very much, and life couldn't be better. We only told everyone later that we'd got hitched. For a while it was just a private thing between Matt and I.

Little did I know that as I said "I do" I was on the verge of entering several years of abusive hell. All in all, Matt would go on to stab me three times in total while we were together, but at the start of our relationship I had no idea that things would turn out like that. After our stint in Manchester we drove off to North Wales and moved in with his Mum. We lived there with her for a while, before going on to live in Birkenhead. My son was living between my Mum's house and his Dad's – my ex's -at that stage.

Matt's Mum was horrible. When he stabbed me the first time, she said,

"What are you moaning for, Nicola, it's only a bloody nick".

She was so unsympathetic and uncaring, even though it was actually a deep gash that he'd made on my face and the blood was everywhere. This incident came about because one day, Matt asked me how many people I'd slept with prior to him. And so I told him – it wasn't that many, you could count the number on two hands – I think I said six. But he went nuts and immediately started messing with one of his chef's knives. He was always very jealous and he couldn't bear the thought of me sleeping with anyone but him. Just that little conversation we'd had had sent him round the bend. The cut he ended up giving me wasn't just a 'nick', it was horrific and deep, and you can still see the scar that was left.

When he stabbed me – just between the eyes - my blood had spattered up the walls, it was literally everywhere. It looked like a massacre had taken place in that room. But his Mum thought that Matt could never do any wrong, so she was no help or support to me whatsoever. And as I soon found out, back then if you went to the police, they didn't listen. I did go and file a report against him and tried to explain what he'd done, but because I'd broken into the house that was in Matt's name to get my clothes back, he ended up pressing charges against me for that. So it turned into a tit-for-tat situation and the police just weren't interested at all in what I had to say. They didn't take me seriously. I've never had no luck with coppers, to be honest. After this particular episode, Matt's abuse just got worse and worse.

Once, when we were in Wales and I'd just come back from a visit to Manchester, Matt discovered that I had more money with me than I'd first admitted to him. This simple fact made him so mad, his face went completely red with anger and suddenly I was shit scared of what he was going to do. He'd had a problem with drugs for a while and was doing a lot of coke back then, and it was making his behaviour really unpredictable but he'd never looked so fucking insanely furious before. He grabbed a shovel and ordered me to get in the car, then he drove us off into the valleys. I remember how dark it was that night, there were bats flying around as we sped down the narrow lanes. My heart was beating so fast I thought I was going to be sick. Eventually, he stopped the car in a wooded area, made me get out and marched me onwards through the trees until we came to a clear patch.

He held a knife to my throat, gave me the spade, and told me to dig my own grave. He said he was going to bury me alive. I honestly thought I was going to die that evening. But I managed to calm him down – it took ages - and eventually we returned to the house. However, that incident turned out to be just the beginning of Matt's abuse. As his mental health and drug use deteriorated, his abusive behaviour towards me escalated.

It got to the point where Matt was kicking off all the time. When we were en route to Birkenhead we stopped at his Dad's house in Flint and we ended up staying there for a bit. One day we had an argument about money and he smashed my face in until it was puffy and sticking out. So I ran into his Dad's bedroom – which was next to ours – looking for help. I ended up on the floor, grabbing his Dad by his trouser legs, trying to get him to see what a state I was in and what his son had done. I desperately wanted his Dad to support me and to stop Matt from doing anything else violent. I was so scared and my face was hurting badly. But his Dad picked me up and put me back in the room with Matt, so that his son could carry on battering me. An hour later, when Matt had worn himself out and had finally decided to leave me alone, his Dad opened our bedroom door and threw a packet of frozen peas at me.

I suppose this was his way of trying to help my massively swollen and bruised face; but he'd already enabled his son's abuse by taking me back into that bedroom. Matt then wanted sex, so I had to sleep with him. I could see myself in the mirror and I couldn't take my eyes off my battered face. And he kept saying, "Come on my little gerbil."

He was laughing at the injuries and puffiness that he'd inflicted on me. I can't even describe how awful that made me feel. All I could think about was how enlarged and damaged my face was while he was shagging me. That night, I crept downstairs after Matt had passed out drunk and went into the bathroom, which was on the ground floor. I climbed out of the window and ran bare foot to the police station. My feet got cut as I legged it over the rough paving slabs but nothing was going to deter me from getting there. I reported what he'd done to the police and I had to phone my Mum to come and pick me up.

Neither of his parents ever supported me when Matt was violent; his Mum thought the sun shone out of his arse, and his Dad had about ten children with ten different women and just didn't put any effort in.

One time, when we were living in Birkenhead, I got to the point where I felt like I'd just had enough of his mood swings, his abusive behaviour and his constant drug use. So I upped and left him, and moved in with my Mum in Manchester. But a little while later, I started having second thoughts. Even though it sounds crazy now, because I still loved him so much at that point I decided to return to Birkenhead and give him another chance.

He'd said all the right things on the phone and I chose to believe that he really meant them this time. That everything was going to be okay. And to be honest, my Mum was a bit sick of me flitting between her house and Matt's; she just wanted me to settle down and stay in one place. So back I went to Birkenhead to be with my husband. But after I got back, we got into an argument and Matt ended up stabbing me again.

He said that I brought this punishment on myself for leaving him, that I shouldn't have done such a thing. I didn't tell my Mum about his latest bit of violence; it was too embarrassing and humiliating. So I just dealt with it myself and somehow managed to crack on and move forwards.

The Loss of Hope

The final straw came when we were living in Birkenhead. I was nine months pregnant with our daughter. Matt had started smoking crack on top of everything else and his mood swings were getting out of control. I was constantly going back to my Mum's, then back to him, always hoping he'd calmed down and that we could lead a more settled life together. But it didn't happen. As I mentioned earlier, he'd always been really jealous of me and other blokes, and accused me of things I'd never done. I'd gone back to my Mum's, needing some rest from his outbursts before the baby was born, when he unexpectedly arrived on her doorstep. I can remember how he dragged me down my Mum's street, battering me.

Before long I had a black eye and bruises all over. Then he started kicking my belly, right where the baby was. In the end my Mum managed to drag him off me, but I knew in my heart that he'd killed our baby. Later on, when I was sitting in the bath trying to calm down, there was no movement at all in my tummy – which was very unusual. Then the baby didn't move all night or the next day, and soon a scan confirmed that she had died. I called her Hope, and I keep her photo with me today. I know it sounds bad, but in the end I was glad that our daughter hadn't made it, because it would have meant that I'd have been tied to Matt forever. And what kind of life would she have had, being brought up around his violent temper? I cried that day, I felt so sad and confused. But I also had a sense of relief.

At the hospital they gave me my own room and induced labour in me every day for a week. Eventually the contractions started; I can remember the labour like it happened yesterday, even though it was twenty one years ago. I had to lie in my bed all day, listening to the cries of healthy babies being born all around me. Matt and his Mum came to visit me, and – for once – his mother was being kind to me and showed me attention. The attention infuriated Matt and, when she'd gone, Matt kicked off and started dragging me around the room by my hair while I was in labour. It was horrendous, but I was too scared of him to tell the nurses. I was so glad when he left and went home.

An African doctor came into the delivery room and broke my waters. And then there was the little old lady who was my midwife. She told me that she'd worked as a midwife all through her adult life. I could tell she felt really awkward – as we both knew that the baby was gone but we had to go through the motions and she just didn't know what to say to me. I had already decided in my head that when the time was right, I was just going to push like my life depended on it, and get the whole thing over and done with. To be honest, I was scared shitless, but I knew it was just a situation that I had to deal with, so I had to get on with it.

I can remember one thing about being in the hospital, as clear as day. There was a girl in there, who'd been in the year above me at school. She was stunning, and her name was Gillian. She had dark curly hair in a concave bob, olive skin, and a perfect figure. Everyone used to envy her. But years after she'd left the school, she'd become hooked on heroin. And there she was in the hospital, giving birth. Her baby came out alive and healthy, but addicted to heroin.

The whole time I was in labour, I had to listen to that baby going through cold turkey while I knew that my daughter was dead inside me. That was incredibly hard to deal with. Gillian's poor baby was screaming so hard, it sounded like it was being tortured. At one point, Gillian left the baby in the hospital, and went out to score some smack. Also, I had to deal with the smell of everyone else's new born babies while I was in there, like the baby shampoo and talc that was being used. I was in my own room at the side of the delivery ward, but those smells still managed to find their way into my room and linger around, which was hard.

The contractions got more and more frequent until eventually my time came, and at that point I pushed as hard as I could. The delivery was actually over really quickly and there were no complications. My daughter – Hope – came out into the world absolutely perfect. But she was dead.

I remember the midwife leaning over and trying to wipe my daughter's face, but as she did so Hope's skin was just peeling away and exposing the blood underneath. The midwife started crying. She turned to me. "I'm sorry," she said. "I can't do this. Her skin is coming off. I'm so sorry."

She picked up my daughter, wrapped her in a blanket, then passed her to me. I placed her on my lap, then just stared at my baby in silence. She was so beautiful. It just looked like she was fast asleep. I felt like I was in a big daze. I must have kept her on my knee, staring at her like that, for over an hour. I was numb; emotionless. What could I do?

Then the nurse came back in and asked me if I wanted to take some photos of Hope before they took her away. I agreed. But what happened next is a memory that I have to deal with every day of my life. It never goes away, but I've just had to learn to live with it. I lifted Hope up so that she could have her photo taken, but at that point her skull collapsed and all the skin on her face became baggy. In order to be able to take a photo of her, the midwife and I had to tuck the skin in on either side of her face – folding it back inside the blanket so that you couldn't see how it really looked. It was like my daughter had a face that didn't have a skull supporting it. The image of her like that will remain in my head until the day I die.

The midwife couldn't stop crying; she didn't know what to do or say to me. I found out later that after that day with me the midwife quit her job. When I left the hospital and went home, I found that a lot of people I knew were avoiding me, because they didn't know what to say about the death of my daughter. They just felt too awkward.

Having Hope, and then having to immediately say goodbye to her, changed me as a person. My attitude became: I don't give a shit about anything in life. This might sound bad, but if anyone around me fell pregnant then I hated them for it. Especially if they were expecting a girl. I could never go near anyone's babies. Also, I made a vow to myself that I've kept ever since: I was never ever going to take shit off any man, ever again.

We held a funeral for our baby, Hope. I couldn't bring myself to carry the coffin – it was as small as a shoebox – and he battered me again because of this. He thought I should have been able to carry the box containing our baby, but I was just too distraught. On top of this, Matt's mood swings were getting worse, and he was having all sorts of people round the house who I didn't like. He was drinking heavily, and at that point I found out that he was smoking crack a lot too. One day, he told me that he wanted to show me something and took me into the kitchen. There was a tub of bicarbonate of soda sitting on the counter. And I knew straight away; it's common knowledge that if you're on coke and you mix it with bicarb or ammonia that's how you make crack. Because all this stuff was messing with his head, his behaviour towards me just got worse and worse.

We had a bad argument one day, over nothing as normal. Something snapped in me, as I watched Matt shouting and ranting. I'd finally had enough, I was ready to move on at last. So I grabbed a black bin bag and shoved as many of my clothes in as I could, then got in the new car that my Mum had bought off a neighbour for me when I was pregnant. I drove straight to Manchester, and went straight to the homeless shelter. Little did I know that I would meet some girls there who would change the direction of my life forever...

Chapter Three
Testing the Waters & Finding my Feet

I'd chosen to go to the homeless shelter in Manchester and not to my Mum's house, because, by this time, she was sick of my coming and going. And, to be honest, I was a grown woman by then. I needed my freedom and independence and staying back with my Mum full time would have been too difficult for both of us at that point. So, I decided to forge my own path ahead in life, by myself.

The people at the homeless office booked me into a shelter called Direct Access in Plymouth Grove. As I arrived outside it, I looked up and saw how high the building was; how many floors it had. I remember how I found a parking space at the back, then walked into the reception area wondering what I'd find. A woman who worked there told me which room I was in, and, as I followed her directions, I found that I had to walk up loads of stairs to get to it since it was on one of the higher floors. On the ground floor, I'd seen a big canteen like one you'd find in a school; later on, I found out that they sold dead cheap meals there for about a pound each – like chips and gravy and apple pie. It looked like a well-run kind of place.

As I went on, with my black bin bag of clothes slung over my shoulder, I saw that there were lounges on each floor where all the residents could socialise together. I also saw some of the other residents walking around; they were proper homeless people with ripped clothes like the ones you might see sitting in shop doorways. There were communal toilets for everyone on each landing and these yellow bins were nailed to the walls everywhere. I looked at them wondering why they were there and what they were for. Later, I found out that there were a lot of smack addicts in the shelter and those bins were for their needles. When I finally reached my room, I opened the door and saw that there was just a sink and a single bed in it. I put my bin bag of clothes down on the bed and arranged the contents from the bag of toiletries that the lady in reception had given me. It was time to settle into my new home!

The whole place smelt of piss. There were a lot of people in there who were alcoholics off the street and they just seemed to wee wherever they felt they needed to; so there was always a very strong odour of stale urine in the air. The corridors smelt of cleaning products, as the staff would continuously mop the floors, trying to hide the smell of stale piss. The canteen at the homeless shelter was definitely the best thing about the place. It smelt exactly like the one at my secondary school. When you sat and had your dinner in there, you would usually be seated next to someone who had accidentally pissed themselves but wasn't aware of it, as they were too out of their nut. But they were mostly nice people in there, they were just lost souls. Ninety percent of them had probably lost everything in their lives, including their homes and families, due to alcohol and addiction problems.

As the days went on, I got friendly with these three girls from my landing. I started watching them; how they acted and where they went, and I began to realise that they had more expensive possessions than most of the other residents in the shelter. I sussed them going out with Reebok Classic trainers on and wearing other pricey things. They were always leaving in taxis together, coming back late, and whispering amongst themselves. Something was going on there and I wanted to find out what it was. So I got friendly with them and asked them where they kept going; eventually, I earned their trust and they opened up to me, explaining that they were going on the beat. They were prostitutes.

On the first day that I'd arrived at the shelter and looked at the contents of the bag of clothes that I'd brought with me, I'd found that in my rush to leave Matt and get to Manchester, I'd only grabbed my clubbing clothes. I had items with me like a purple PVC skirt and a PVC vest top to match, and lace see-through pants with a little bra top to match. I couldn't wear any of these clothes; I'd just had a baby – Hope – so I'd put on weight, and anyway, even if they did fit me, you wouldn't wear clothes like that to go out in the day, would you?

Once I became friends with these three girls, I told them that they might as well get some wear out of my clubbing clothes – as there was no chance that I was going to. I thought it would help them to look better than they did and, therefore, help them to make more money when they went out looking for punters. I also offered them a deal; I said that if they each gave me twenty quid a day, I would drive them to the beat where they worked near the bus station, wait until they'd done whatever they were doing, give them a lift to go and score their drugs and, finally, take them back to the refuge. All the girls accepted, which I was happy about, as it meant I'd found a way to make a bit of money.

So the next time the three of them were about to leave the shelter, I gave them my bag of clothes and we sorted out who was going to wear what. One of them had the purple PVC outfit, another had the white lace leggings and the white lace top, and I can't recall what the third girl wore. Then I took them on their beat. They were all a bit older than I was at the time; they were all in their thirties and junkies, whereas I was still only twenty seven. You could tell they were on drugs as their teeth were a mess. I remember the time when one of the girls had robbed a chemist and she showed me a big bag of tablets that looked like sweets. That night the girls sat in the lounge that was on our floor and took a bunch of tablets out of the bag – they looked like pick-n-mix – and put them on a spoon. They heated them up and then injected them. I'd never seen anything like it before.

My deal with the three of them worked out well for a while, and I used to regularly take them out to work and score. Then one day, I'd taken one of the girls – Bonita – out on her own. She went and had sex with a customer but when she came back to me she was rattling – it was clear that she needed a bag of heroin to work otherwise she wouldn't be able to get through the rest of the night. So I took her to go and score and then she went back out working. I was fascinated by all this; I'd never seen anyone doing this before and I'd never seen them heating up heroin on spoons and injecting or smoking it either.

Some people at the shelter smoked crack too. And there were a lot of drunks there too, people who were always collapsing outside. There was never a dull moment. The deal I had with the girls was working out well for me as well as for them; I was getting sixty quid a day for driving them around so I was able to buy petrol, food as also toiletries of my own and clothes that actually fit me.

Anyway, on the night that I took Bonita out by herself, when we got back to the shelter, she didn't give me her twenty quid like the girls usually did. So I asked her for my money and she said no, she'd give me some drugs instead. The other two girls looked at her oddly, as they knew I didn't take anything. It got to the point where – as she was refusing to pay me – we started fighting. I was dragging her around the room by her hair and we were both screaming at each other when the staff came upstairs to find out what was going on.

The upshot of the incident was that I ended up leaving the shelter after only a couple of months of living there. But I wasn't going to let a little episode like that break me, I had to crack on – like I had been doing all my life. So I went and stayed at my Mum's house that night. And, on the next day,

I went to the homeless office in Urmston near Old Trafford; I was determined to find somewhere else to live as soon as I could. I found out that back then, you didn't really have to go on a waiting list for a house if you asked for one in a shit hole area, as they'd just give it to you. So I asked for a two bed house on Oak Road in Partington and they gave it to me straight away. I was delighted.

When I arrived at the house with my belongings, I found that it was at the end of a row, directly facing a line of shops. One of those businesses was called the Partington Project – it was a charity shop. It looked like a good place for me to start shopping for essentials for the house, as I didn't have a lot of money at the time, and I couldn't afford to spend much of what I did have. There was nothing in the house when I got it – it was completely empty, no furniture at all - so I went over to the Partington Project and bought a bed from them for about twenty quid. It was a divan, and I really liked it, although I didn't even have a duvet or anything else to go with it at that stage. But when I got it home, I found that it was ridden with fleas, because when I woke up the next morning, there were black dots all over me and I was horrified to find that that's exactly what they were!

Now, one thing that I'm not is a thief or a shoplifter. In the years gone by, I had wished that I'd had the balls to nick stuff, but I never did. I've never been like that. If I'm in a shop with a friend and she robs a lipstick, I walk out in disgust. But that one time, when I found out that my bed – and then, subsequently, all my clothes – had become riddled with fleas, I did have to rob some flea spray from Boots because it was so expensive - it was about twenty quid or something - and I just didn't have that sort of money to spare. After I got home and I was spraying the bed, it dawned on me that I just couldn't live like this for much longer. I had absolutely nothing. I couldn't even furnish the house.

I desperately needed to start bringing some money in, or I just couldn't see how I was going to be able to keep going. Then a memory popped into my head, of a conversation that I'd had with a friend, about a girl we both knew – Amy – who worked at a brothel called *The Edwardian* in Manchester. My mate had told me that Amy was earning silly money working as a prostitute. It was at that moment that I decided to give *The Edwardian* a call. *After all*, I'd thought at the time, *what do I have to lose?* Maybe my time driving the three girls around at the shelter had made me remember this information, I'm not really sure. But that's how I came to work in my first brothel.

After I was given a "working interview" and gave Jonathan a blowjob while he did poppers, I was very pleased when I was officially given a job at *The Edwardian*. You could still smoke inside it back then and I can remember the reception area and the rooms always being cloudy and stinking heavily of cigarette smoke. The toilet and the girls' changing room round the back, however, often smelt of rotting fish because that's what heroin smells like. As in any parlour, there was also the constant sound of beds banging – which indicated that customers were going for it hammer and tongs. You could also frequently hear customers and girls screaming with delight as they climaxed. Some were quiet when they did this, while others were very noisy!

My initial plan was to just work at *The Edwardian* for a month while I furnished my house. In just three weeks, I'd kitted the place out and my home was now full of new IKEA furniture, which I loved. I'd painted the walls nicely too, had the garden done, and had a brand new hire car on my drive which I paid a hundred pound a week for. I thought I was something I wasn't. I was made up. And then to be honest, after a month at *The Edwardian*, I found the money I was earning too addictive to just give up. I wasn't ready to let go of the good lifestyle that I was beginning to have. So I kept working. And started to meet some really interesting people…

After my first customer at *The Edwardian*, Jonathan, I can remember another one that stands out as clear as day. His name was Graham. I remember meeting him in the reception area for the first time and he asked me if I specialised. So I told him that I did oral but not anal. He booked me for an hour.

"Can you take Graham into the Gold room for an hour please, Nicole?" Tracy the receptionist said. "No problem," I said, and took my customer into the room that directly faced the reception. It had a gorgeous interior, with a massive sold wood king-size bed, a power shower, and loads of nice accessories. At the bottom of the bed was a two seater jacuzzi that had mirrors all around it. After I'd settled Graham in there, I went back to the reception to see Tracy.

"Now listen Nicole," she whispered, leaning forwards over the reception desk. "Graham is a very good customer. We call him Gold Room Graham because he always books that room and will never take any other. If he likes you, he will probably book you again. Sometimes he pays for the whole night. So make sure he's happy with his service." She gave me a pack of condoms and I walked back towards the Gold room. When I got there, I found that Graham was lying face down on the bed. All I could see was his fat white back, his receding hair, his huge spotty arse and his stumpy legs.

"Take your clothes off please, Nicole," Graham said. "And give me a massage with baby lotion." His voice was stern. So I took my clothes off slowly, and flung them on the floor. Then I walked to the wooden bedside table, grabbed the baby lotion, and then climbed on to the bed next to Graham. At that point, it was still early days for me at The Edwardian, and as I looked at his body lying there I remember thinking, *what the bleeding hell am I doing here?* Then I just thought *Sod it. I'm only doing this for a month to furnish my house, so what does it matter? Give your head a wobble Nicola and act like you know how to give someone a massage.*

I squirted some of the oily lotion on to my hand and began to rub it into Graham's back very slowly. I was trying to do it in a way that I thought a professional masseuse might do it. Graham seemed to be enjoying it, and I could hear him making soft grunting noises into the pillow. Then – all of a sudden – he flipped over on to his back. I bent my body forwards, trying to hide my sloppy stretch mark ridden stomach.

"Can you massage between my thighs?" Graham said.

"'Course I can, lovely," I replied. I started rubbing the lotion between his legs, making sure that I was getting closer to his penis all the time. He was loving all the teasing; he kept trying to thrust his now very hard cock towards my hands, but I just giggled and playfully moved my hands away. After a while, when he'd got to the point where I knew he just couldn't take it any more, I gently put my hands round his rock hard dick and climbed in between his legs. Then I started to stroke my face with his cock, rubbing his big, hard, shiny bell end across my lips in a provocative manner.

"Oh Nicole, you tease," Graham said, his voice a delighted squeak. "Put it in your mouth and suck it please."

I just giggled, and thought to myself: *not yet, you're getting teased to death*. I slowly licked up and down the sides of his stiff prick, and each time I got to the top I would go to put his bell end in my mouth, look him in the eye, then shake my head and stop. When I knew he couldn't take it any more, I put my mouth round the end of his cock and started sucking it up and down, making sure that my mouth was soaking with spit. It was dribbling out of my mouth and down Graham's hard prick and he was loving it. I could feel him starting to pulsate in my mouth, then his balls went tight and I knew that any minute he was going to explode. All of a sudden he let out a roar and blew his load into my mouth. I looked him in the eyes and smiled.

"Wow Nicole," he said, exhaling. "That was amazing. I want to book you for longer."

"Why, thank you," I said with a grin.

Graham leant over the side of the bed, grabbed his trousers and withdrew his wallet from one of the pockets.

"I'm going to have you all night," he said. I glanced at the clock; it was nearly midnight and I was working until five that morning. So Graham booking me for the rest of the night – i.e. five more hours - meant he was about to give the receptionist three hundred and fifty pounds. The fee for the Gold room back then was seventy pound an hour; the girl got forty and the house took thirty.

After I'd taken Graham's money to Tracy in reception, I went back into the room and spent the rest of my shift with him. To be fair, it was an absolute doddle. He had already come once and it soon became obvious that he couldn't manage a second time. He just wanted female company and a cuddle really. We lay there on the bed together for hours, just talking. I found out that he was an accountant who lived in Leeds with his mother. He'd never had a proper long-term girlfriend before, which was mainly due to his controlling Mum. He told me that he'd been coming to *The Edwardian* for years. He'd even lost his virginity there when he was in his late forties. Although he seemed happy enough with himself, I remember thinking that it was a sad life that he'd lived; never having had a partner and even having to still answer to his parents in his forties. But as he didn't know any different, he seemed all right, he was content enough with his lot.

The Ominous Menace of Drugs

I got into a routine at *The Edwardian* working three set shifts a week and I was loving both the job and the money. After getting to know some of the other girls who worked there, I realised that there were all sorts of reasons for someone to get into prostitution. Some got the money so they could go and buy drugs, some used their wages to support their children.

And some girls just did it because it was an easy, lavish lifestyle. One common denominator that I discovered among all the prostitutes that I talked to was that all of them had been through some sort of domestic violence situation in our lives. It's a strange but true fact. I don't think I've ever come across a working girl who doesn't have some sort of history of domestic abuse.

While I was working there, I met some really lovely girls who came from all walks of life. Making the decision to become a prostitute doesn't mean you have to come from a drug-ridden, poverty-filled background, although I'm aware that that's how lots of people who are outside the sex industry bubble perceive the situation. One girl who I worked with there – Madison (her working name) – had been private school educated and her family was a very well-to-do one from Huddersfield. She was absolutely stunning, only eighteen years old, with long, straight blonde hair that went right down to her bum. She was an athlete, a perfect size ten, with a peachy bottom, a tiny waist and small 32C boobs. She was an ex BMX bike rider for Great Britain, so you can imagine – she was perfectly toned.

When I met Madison during her first Friday night shift, to be honest, I was a bit jealous of her, because she was so beautiful. Prostitution is a very competitive business and it is natural for envious feelings to arise if a girl is younger, prettier and busier than you. But I knew that it wasn't Madison's fault that she was so attractive, plus she had a lovely personality. She ended up working the shifts that I did, so we became quite close, although I never bothered meeting up with her outside the job. The fact that she was always so quick to leave at the end of each shift caught my attention, although at the time I didn't realise that it was because she was hiding a dark secret. It took me months before I sussed out what was up with her.

Because we were both blonde, we would get booked together for lots of the two-girl jobs. One guy that used to book us all the time was a very famous Member of Parliament (MP). He would like to have us perform oral sex on each other and then on him. We would both laugh at him when he wasn't looking, and when he told us to go down on each other we would pull our hair over our faces so that he couldn't see that we weren't actually licking each other out.

Then I would straddle his face while Madison would mount his cock and put it in her pussy. She would pretend she'd actually put it up her arse and then she would tense her fanny so that he was none the wiser. He'd usually come in seconds, thinking he was fucking her up the arse. Madison would then be buzzing because we were allowed to charge customers extras for anal. She would always get an extra fifty quid off him.

Looking back, I'm surprised that nobody recognised that MP going in and out of *The Edwardian* all the time. I'm not really into politics, but he was so well known that I knew who he was straight away, as soon as I saw him. To be honest, he was quite a nice person; once you got chatting to him he was very down to earth. He would tell us loads of stories about his university days and about all the drug-fuelled parties he'd attended. I still giggle to myself when I see photos of him in the newspapers and think: *You've licked Madison's and my cunt on numerous occasions, lol.*

Madison was a really busy lady; some days she was booked up solid. I remember wondering what she spent her money on because she never seemed to have any left when she came into work. She never brought any cash with her to pay for her taxi, she always had to borrow the fare from the receptionist. She never bought any new work outfits and she always wore the same tatty underwear. When we ordered food, she would never eat anything. Looking back, I should have clicked straight away what the problem with Madison was, but it took me months to work it out, and by then it was too late…

One day Ethel (the boss) was doing the books and was working out what Madison had earned that year. It was more than what a prime minister would have earned: over a hundred thousand pounds! And, that didn't include all the extras she got paid for in the room – and Madison did every extra possible: anal, rimming, swallowing and towards the end, she did bareback sex (without a condom). It was heart-breaking what went on to happen to her.

I remember how each time she came into work she would look slimmer and slimmer and her skin seemed to turn very grey. Her gorgeous natural blonde hair started looking dry and brittle, her finger nails were always dirty, and she started having dark circles around her eyes.

One day when I came into work, I already had a customer waiting for me in the room. I needed to go to the toilet quickly and put a sponge up myself (a prostitute wears a sponge during sex when they are on their period so that they don't bleed, and the customer is none the wiser – that way you don't have to have any time off work). Madison had been in the toilet for ages, and I was aware that my customer was waiting for me and I had been shouting at Madison to hurry up for ages. In the end, I just opened the door and walked straight into the cubicle. Her face told me how gutted she was that I had seen what I had; she was trying to hide what was in her hand, but it was too late. I'd seen the needle and the spoon. Madison was a heroin addict.

I felt really embarrassed by what I'd just seen and so was she. It was a most awkward moment. I can still remember it now, the smell of burning heroin in that toilet; it reeked like rotten fish. I felt so gutted by what I'd just seen. *Why was she doing it?* I thought to myself. *Madison was the prettiest girl at The Edwardian, what was she thinking of, doing heroin?* I couldn't believe it. I just couldn't get my head round it.

Over the next few months, Madison's health got worse and worse, and her looks deteriorated. All of her teeth turned into short black stumps and she started wearing a cardigan and long black stockings during every shift to hide the amount of needle marks on her body. Then she started walking with a limp because she developed an abscess in her groin from all the injecting and it stank because it got infected. She confided in me that she'd started taking heroin after an ex-boyfriend – who was a lot older than her – introduced her to it.

He also got her on to crack. It just shows that a person can come from any background and end up on drugs. Madison had come from very loving, privileged circumstances, but had just got in with the wrong people as she'd grown up. Watching her deteriorate like that was really awful.

Our boss didn't give a shit about Madison once she'd hit rock bottom. Before that, I'd always thought Ethel was okay as she'd never had a problem with me. But looking back, it was really because I was always busy and making her money, nothing else. Ethel was all for Madison when she first arrived and was getting lots of business, but once she'd gone downhill and her numbers dropped, she changed her opinion. Madison no longer interested Ethel. I understand that business is business, but, at the same time, human beings are human beings. God knows, maybe my attitude is wrong. Anyway, eventually Ethel got rid of Madison due to her no longer being financially viable and the poor girl also looked so bad in the end that she simply wasn't saleable.

Madison ended up going from parlour to parlour and, in the end, she was living and working on the streets. She died at the age of twenty eight from drugs and alcohol. I remember how she rang me up asking for a job about a year before she died. I had my own place by then but I didn't give her any work because I knew what a mess she was in. I feel guilty about that now in some ways because when she asked for work my attitude was the same as Ethel's. I should have tried to help her, maybe not with a job but with sorting herself out. I often think about what would have happened if I had done something. Would she be alive now? But unfortunately, I can't change the past.

After I'd met Madison, I began to realise just how big a part drugs could play in the lives of sex workers and their clients...

Chapter Four
Perverse Men & Willing Addicts

Now that I look back at my time in *The Edwardian*, I can see that there came a point where all the "normal" girls seemed to vanish. When I say normal, I'm referring to the ones who didn't take heavy drugs like crack or heroin. At one point, I was pretty much the only non-drug addict on each shift. In the end, it became a regular day for me to be on the toilet putting a sponge inside of myself, while three other girls - who were working the same shift – were crowded together on the bathroom floor, heating up spoons and sharing needles. It was weird watching them inject themselves with heroin. They were all okay with me – we had no trouble with each other – and I figured that what they wanted to spend their money on was their business. What did bother me, however, was the type of customers they got as druggies, and the sort of things those customers would have them doing for extra money.

Some guys - who seem like normal, married, family men - are actually sick in the head when it comes to what they want to do with prostitutes. And the crazy thing is that the real world – outside the parlour bubble – is totally oblivious to all this. They have no idea what's really going on behind the brothels closed doors. I always felt lucky because I was never addicted to those hard types of drugs, so never felt compelled to go the extra mile to get a few more quid. But when someone is rattling and will do anything to get their next fix, its horrendous watching them being taken advantage of whilst the sick customer is also getting a sexual kick out of it.

For example, there was this accountant who the other girls called 'Peter the Beater'. He was a fat, dumpy, ugly guy who was about fifty years old. He had dark, receding hair, a huge nose, jagged teeth and a sweaty forehead. He was always suited and booted, and carried a large leather briefcase wherever he went. I'd been reliably informed that he was a good tipper (the girls said he would give them an extra fifty or a hundred pounds at the end of each service, depending on how happy he was with it). However, he only ever booked me once, because when I was with him, I immediately realised the sort of guy that he was and refused to do most of the acts he was demanding. He booked me for one hour in the Penthouse (the most expensive room in *The Edwardian*). I left him there to shower, then walked back into the room. I was surprised to see that there were now loads of objects arrayed all over the bed, that included a pair of nipple clamps, a paddle, some home-made suction things to go on your nipples, a sharp metal roller type thing on a stick, rope, duct tape, a pump that you put inside a woman's vagina to stretch it, and some sharp knife things.

As I looked at all these objects my head started freaking out, and I asked Peter what they were for. He looked at me with an evil smirk on his face and said:

"You've been a very, very naughty girl, Nicole."

What the fuck? I thought.

"Okay, what do I have to do?" I said, my voice coming out quiet.

"If you let me punish you," Peter said, coming closer to me. "I'll give you lots of money at the end."

"Okay," I said. I was wondering what he was about to do…

Peter lunged forwards and grabbed me by my hair, while telling me that I was a dirty slag. It didn't hurt, so I thought that maybe I could work with this situation – as it wasn't too bad so far. He then pulled me towards the bed and grabbed these nipple clamps and squeezed them hard on to my nipples.

"Ouch," I said, moving away. "That's too hard."

I could immediately see that he was pissed off with me because I wasn't playing ball with him; he wanted to punish me as much as he liked without me complaining too much.

"Do you take a spanking?" He said.

"Yes," I said, feeling wary. "But not too hard."

He told me to lie face down on the bed, then he slapped my ass really brutally.

"Hey, that's too hard," I said, sitting up.

I could tell by the purple colour spreading across his face that he was now livid with me. We agreed to continue the service with my just sucking his cock, but he didn't come. At the end of the hour, he chucked me twenty quid and said:

"Thanks Nicole. Can you go downstairs and ask the receptionist to send someone else in please?"

"No problem," I said, going over to the door. To be honest, I was glad to get out of that room. I didn't give a shit about his big tip; I had my boundaries, and there was no way I was going to let a guy hurt me just so I could earn a few extra quid. So I went down and told a girl called Samantha that she had an hours booking with Peter the Beater. She was made up.

"Yay, a one hundred pound tip for me," she said, as she made her way upstairs. *Fuck that*, I thought to myself, watching her back view disappear.

Sad Story of Samantha

Samantha was one of the loveliest girls there at that time. She was in her twenties back then, quite chubby with jet black curly hair and the most piercing blue eyes I'd ever seen. She wasn't exactly stunning, but there was definitely something alluring about her. With me, she was always very clingy and touchy feely, she would always come over for a cuddle like she was craving love and affection. She came from Newton Heath and had had a shit upbringing as her mother was a junkie. Her brother had died and she'd never got over his death.

When he'd passed away Samantha's Mum had got her hooked on heroin, telling her that it would help blank out her pain. With an upbringing like that, she'd never stood a chance in life, and the sad thing is – none of it was her fault. I really liked Samantha; she was such a happy and bubbly person to be around with. Although, don't get me wrong – she was also a cunt; if she had the opportunity to rob you blind, then she would have. But she was just such a likeable character.

So, anyway, off Samantha went, up the stairs to service Peter the Beater. I can remember how – a short while later – heavy banging noises started coming from the room they were in. *What the bloody hell are they doing in there?* I thought, hoping that everything was okay. About forty five minutes later, Peter came down the stairs. He was sweating even more than normal.

"Can I pay for my room please, Tracy?" He said to the receptionist.

"Course, Peter," she said, looking up at him. "Is everything okay for you today? It's just that I've noticed that you're leaving a little earlier than normal."

"Oh, splendid," Peter said with a big grin. "Both the ladies I had today were fantastic. As always."

I watched as he sorted out his bill and left the building. Five minutes later, Samantha walked slowly down the stairs. I could see straight away that she had a black eye and that there was blood dripping down the side of her face.

"What the fuck?" I said, walking over to her quickly. "What the hell has he done to you?"

She gave a smirk, and said in a blasé way:

"Peter's just given me two hundred quid because I let him smack my face off the steps to the Jacuzzi for a while."

I just stared at her, my mouth open. What a cunt, I thought. Peter knew that Samantha was a drug addict, and he'd just totally taken advantage of her needs. He'd come in, physically abused her, then walked out of *The Edwardian* quite happy, off to see his wife and kids back home. When I'd clocked him at the reception, he'd been acting like nothing significant had just happened. Samantha's injuries meant nothing to him. Every day, I realised, he must just sit in his accountancy office, with no one around him knowing what sick, seedy kicks he liked to get in his spare time. In reality, he was just taking advantage of vulnerable people, getting some sort of perverse sexual pleasure out of hurting them. Just thinking about him knocked me sick. After that incident, every time Peter the Beater came into *The Edwardian*, I would just give him the dirtiest look, then walk straight out of the room.

The Morbid Tale of Melissa

I can remember another time, when a different girl – Melissa, who was also a druggie – had an encounter with him. This girl looked like a drug addict, she was a complete mess. She had a tiny child-like figure, long red frizzy hair, an old haggard face and false teeth. One afternoon, Peter the Beater walked into *The Edwardian*, and he booked Melissa for three hours, so off she went up to the Penthouse Room with him. Shortly after they'd gone upstairs, we heard a bit of banging coming from that room, but not as much as when he'd taken Samantha up there that time. After three hours, Peter came down to reception and said goodbye to Tracy before leaving the building.

The fact that he would always come down before the girl when he'd done something bad to her upstairs had already got my attention, thanks to his behaviour on previous occasions. Maybe he didn't want the girl to come down first in case he felt embarrassed when other people saw the injuries that he'd inflicted on her? Who knows.

Shortly after he'd gone, Melissa made her way down the stairs. Immediately, my eyes went to the blood that was dripping down her arms. But her face was happy, in fact she was grinning from ear to ear.

"I've got two hundred pound," she said, brandishing the money that Peter had given her in the air. "He got me to let him slash my arms with a razor blade," she went on, in answer to my enquiring look. The way she said it was so casual, so blasé, like she didn't even care what he'd done to her. I couldn't believe it, Peter had done it again. That sick cunt had brought in a razor blade, cut up her arms, then chucked her two hundred quid for the pleasure of doing it. There was something seriously wrong with this guy's head. I often used to wonder if he ever did any of his sick, perverted practices outside our parlour. The chances are that Peter wasn't even his real name; most of our customers – like the girls who worked there – used false names. It got to the point with his behaviour that out of all the customers I've ever met in the sex industry, he was one of the ones that I hated the most. He was fucked in the head; it made me want to throw up when I saw the pleasure that he derived from seriously injuring vulnerable girls, who were only letting him practice sadism on them in order to feed their drug habits. Addiction is a disease and these girls needed someone to help them, not to abuse them.

Exploited Emily

I remember another – very young - girl who used to work at *The Edwardian*, called Emily. She turned up one day with another girl called Fay, and when I first saw them together I was taken aback because they made such an odd pair of friends. You wouldn't put them together, they were like chalk and cheese. Fay was a lot older than Emily and, I could instantly tell, just from looking at her, that she was a heavy drug user. She was painfully thin, with exceptionally white skin, blonde hair and dark bags under her eyes. She looked like a living corpse, to be honest. Whereas Emily was the polar opposite; she was extremely young with brown hair, flawless skin, a perfect size ten and a healthy bit of weight on her.

When these two started work at *The Edwardian*, Fay never became very busy with customers, she didn't make a lot of money there. Whereas Emily was the opposite; she was booked up solid. And I think money was the connection that Fay had with Emily. I got the feeling that Fay used her younger friend because the money that Emily earned help pay for both their drug habits. It was rumoured in the parlour that the two had met in a children's home in Rochdale and that Fay had got Emily into heroin and prostitution. How true this is I don't know, but the whole thing about the two of them was very fishy.

Over the next few months, Emily deteriorated dramatically; her heroin habit got worse and worse and as a result her looks faded. She went the exact same way as Madison did and it was horrible to watch it happening all over again. I've seen the same transpire with other girls since; the more money they make, the worse their drug use gets. It's so sad to witness because you just feel so helpless; there's not much you can do to stop them from falling into the hole as they'd never stop taking drugs just because you asked them to.

As Emily hit rock bottom, she started doing more extras in the rooms with customers, including bare back. Our boss, Ethel, didn't give a shit about the girls' health as long as they were making money for her. All she cared about were the high numbers next to each of the girls' names on her sheet; if you were bringing in the cash, she would turn a blind eye to what you got up to in the rooms, even if it meant you were harming yourself. Her attitude was wrong, so wrong. To this day, I often wondered what happened to Emily and where she ended up. One day, she and Fay just stopped coming to *The Edwardian*, and I've never heard from them or seen them since. Chances are they are either working the streets or dead now; and I wouldn't like to put money on which one of those outcomes is more likely.

In the Family too...

One day, my cousin Gina came round to see me and said that she would like me to help her get work at *The Edwardian*. She's the same cousin who had come with my Nana and I to Pontins all those years ago. I think it was because she'd seen me buying all my new clothes and things since I started working there and basically wanted a piece of this. I kept warning her that the job was addictive because of the money and that because of this it wasn't a good industry to get involved in but she wouldn't listen. She was adamant that she wanted to start work at the parlour. She thought she would make a great prostitute because she'd always been very promiscuous with men in the past. She had five children with different men and had always had a carefree attitude towards sex. So I ended up getting her a shift. But looking back now, I really wish I hadn't...

The money that Gina started making at *The Edwardian* really changed her. From my work as a prostitute, I've learnt that once a person starts earning good money, it can change everything about them. People either become givers or takers when they're wealthy and unfortunately Gina became a taker. The more money she made, the greedier and more selfish she became. Then she started gambling and also got into snorting cocaine. It was horrible to watch such a change taking place in my cousin. After she'd worked at the parlour for a while, she'd earned thousands of pounds, but her kids never saw any of it.

Her mum – my aunt – didn't know that Gina worked as a prostitute, so Gina would always manipulate her to get money out of her, pretending she was still poor. Her mum ended up paying for everything for her and her kids.

Gina soon became overly obsessed with money. She always hated the fact that I was busier than her at *The Edwardian* and had more customers; she was also jealous about the fact that I bought nice things with what I earned. But the thing is, she could have done the same as me and she could have invested her money wisely. She just got too grasping and selfish and her newly found wealth blinded her. Now, twenty years later, she's got nothing to show for all the years that she's worked as a prostitute; she never used her money to build a positive life for herself. Today, she's a crack addict and no parlour will take her on as she's robbed everyone blind over the years. The thing is, Gina could have had a great life. She could have had everything that she wanted but greed and drugs got the better of her. It's heart breaking to see the state that she's in now. To be honest, I wish I'd never introduced her to the job. But hey, we can't change our past, we can only choose which way our future goes.

Chapter Five
A Jamaican Farewell

There was a white Jamaican guy who would book me all the time when I was working at *The Edwardian*. He would always go for an hour in an expensive room, which meant more money for me. So, even though I instinctively didn't like the man, I put up with him because business is business and, at the end of the day, I had to earn my living. This guy was probably in his forties back then. He was quite tall and thick set but not fat. He was white skinned, with black facial features, and had afro hair. The only part of his body that was black was his fairly big cock. When he spoke to me, it was with a Jamaican accent. He only ever arrived at *The Edwardian* in the early evenings, or during the day time, and always chose to go into a room with one girl on her own.

Once I was in the room with him, I found him so full of himself. So arrogant. He would pose in different positions, while staring at himself in the mirror, loudly admiring himself and telling me what an amazing body he had. To be honest, I would just agree with him, as I had to get on with the booking and there was no point in saying anything else. After all, he was paying me to make him feel good.

When he fucked me, he was quite forceful. He would lie on top of me and hold my arms behind my head as he penetrated my vagina. But this was nothing I couldn't handle; by then I was used to all sorts. I remember just lying there as he pounded me, thinking: *For fuck's sake, hurry up and come will you?* He'd booked me on many occasions over several months and I didn't think anything bad of him; in my opinion he was just a bit of a pompous twat who liked to be dominating. I knew how he liked his service and everything was going along as normal.

One night, I was working a late shift in *The Edwardian* and this guy came in. I couldn't help noticing how much later he'd arrived than usual. On this occasion, unusually, he booked me together with a busty mixed-race girl called Kelly. The receptionist told us that we both needed to go to a room upstairs for an hour with him. Before we went up, the guy asked me and Kelly if we fancied having a drink with him. This was unusual behaviour – he'd never asked me this before – and I thought: *Bloody hell, he's splashing the cash tonight; two girls and a bottle of champagne, he never goes for all that.* But hey, who was I to complain? As long as I got paid for giving him a good service, it would be happy days. We agreed.

Kelly and I walked up the stairs together, holding our drinks in our hands and giggling, wondering what this guy wanted us to get up to. Once we were in the room, we both plonked ourselves on the big, king sized bed. Mr Jamaica poured us both another glass of champers and then he started to get undressed. Our glasses were only small champagne flutes, so we knocked the drink back pretty quickly.

The man looked at us. "Have another drink," he said, in his strong Jamaican accent. We weren't about to complain about his offer, we were both due to work through the whole night, and when a girl has a drink or two the whole night tends to fly by a lot quicker. So Kelly and I filled up our glasses and had some more. Looking back, this guy seemed to be wanting to rush us to drink, but at the time we didn't think anything of this. Each time we'd drained our glasses, he couldn't fill them up again quick enough. He kept doing this until the very last drop had been drained from the bottle.

After that, he had us both lie on the bed together – naked – while he fingered us at the same time. He would take his finger out of Kelly's pussy and put in in my mouth, and vice versa. By that stage we were both half pissed, but definitely still had our faculties about us. We knew what was going on and what we were doing. After the guy had done this for a while, he got above me, pulled my legs apart and tried to put his hard, black cock into my pussy with no condom on it. Fortunately, I was still with it enough at this stage to realise what he was trying to do. I sat up a bit.

"Hey, what the fuck are you doing?" I shouted at him.

"Come on Nicole," he said. "You know you like the black cock." He tried to thrust himself between my legs again.

"Get off me," I said with a scream, managing to somehow slide my body out from underneath him. The next thing I know, is that Maggie – the receptionist who was on that night – was outside the door, shouting:

"Kelly, Nicole, your time is up."

"Thank fuck for that," I said, giving Mr Jamaica the dirtiest look ever. Kelly and I quickly got dressed and went back downstairs.

At that point, the receptionist ushered me straight into another booking. This time it was with an Asian guy. And that fact is about all I can remember about the customer, his ethnicity, and the fact that as soon as I started sucking his cock I threw up the Doner kebab that I'd had earlier for dinner. My puke went all over his dick.

"Nicole, what the fuck has been going on in there?" Maggie screamed, after the customer left the room and went and found her, with sick all over his cock.

"Oh Maggie," I managed, heaving myself off the bed and wiping my mouth. "I need to go home. I don't feel well at all."

Maggie was livid with me when she heard this. It was a busy night, and if I went home it would leave her with a body down, which meant less customers being serviced, and, therefore, less money coming in. Maggie's bonus system was based on how many happy customers left the building, so my going home early would negatively impact her wages for the evening. But she had to agree with me as I couldn't exactly stay and be sick over more customers. I felt awful leaving her like this, but what else could I do?

What happened next was truly awful. I remember exiting *The Edwardian* and getting into my car. I know I shouldn't have done this – what with the champagne I'd drunk – and I don't make a habit of driving while under the influence. But I was feeling so sick, all I wanted to do was to get home. I can remember reversing my car out of the parking space – it must have been about midnight at this point - but that was literally it. Everything after that was a total blank.

The next thing I knew, I was waking up with a blanket over my head. I reached up and pulled it off, and bright daylight streamed into my eyes. It took me a while to get my bearings, but as I looked around, I realised that I was behind the steering wheel of my car. The driver's side door was wide open and the engine was running. *What the absolute fuck?*

I gradually worked out that my car and I were sitting on the slip road off the M60 motorway near Barton Bridge. I had absolutely no memory of driving there. At that point, I realised that the Jamaican guy must have spiked Kelly and me with a date rape drug the night before. He must have put it in the champagne; no wonder he was so keen for us to keep drinking the stuff. He must have thought that he'd carefully calculated everything. And he had; all except the time it took for the date rape drug to kick in.

He must have been so excited, drugging us both up with the expectation of abusing us. Jesus, with him doing that and my getting into my car, I could have easily killed someone while I was driving – God forbid. I later found out that Kelly had also been poorly after our booking with Mr Jamaica. She'd had to get a taxi back to her house much earlier than usual that night.

It was such a horrible experience. I slowly made my way home and crawled into bed, wondering what the fuck had happened and how I'd come to be on that slip road. I remember Ethel the boss phoning me later in the day.

"What the fuck went on in here last night?" She said into my ear, her tone loud and sharp. I told her all about Mr Jamaica drugging me and Kelly up, and how he tried to force bareback on us. And I explained to her how I'd woken up on the motorway, disorientated and distressed. But Ethel wasn't interested in what I was saying. She only seemed to be bothered about how many customers we'd lost her the previous evening. Her attitude really annoyed me, to be honest. Because even though Mr Jamaica had done this to us, Ethel still allowed him to come into the building and book in with the girls. I mean, what the fuck? But hey, you live and learn with people. I'd never treat one of the girls who work for me now like that.

And, as for our date rape hood, that was it - bye, bye, Mr Jamaica - I have had enough of you. I would never touch you with a barge pole thereafter!

Chapter Six
Tricks and Treats

There were a lot of big personalities who came through the doors of *The Edwardian* while I worked there. And our boss, Ethel, was one of them. Some of the other girls didn't like her, but I personally didn't mind her back then. She would have been in her fifties when I was working for her. I can remember what she looked like then, as clear as day; she had dark, straight hair and was very slim – probably a size eight. To be fair, she looked well for her age.

She'd had a lot of surgery done, including a face lift, eye bags removal, a boob job and Botox, but she looked good with all that. Some people can go over the top with surgery and end up looking hideous. But Ethel just looked natural, like she'd been lucky enough to age well. She was always well-groomed when she came into the parlour and all the clothes she wore were designer. She had a strong Oldham accent – "*You all right cock?*" – type of voice. Back then she smoked heavily and always smelt of Silk Cut cigarettes as well as Angel perfume.

Ethel had started out at *The Edwardian* as a receptionist. Initially, she'd worked for the chap who owned the place, Barry. Ethel was different back then; it was like she was one of the girls. When she worked on reception she would come into the rooms some times and watch while we were servicing a customer, and – on occasion - even got her boobs out for ten quid. But when Barry finished with his wife and got divorced, Ethel seized the opportunity and quickly stepped into his ex's still warm shoes. She started dating Barry and stopped working as the receptionist. Shortly after that, she became the manager of *The Edwardian*. But unfortunately, the money that Ethel began earning changed her, as it does with so many other people. I didn't actually have a problem with the person who she became, as she was always fair with me.

I just thought that the attitude that she developed with the other girls and the receptionists was wrong in a lot of ways. Basically, once she married Barry, Ethel acted as though she was better than everyone else. It was sad watching her become obsessed with money. I've never understood why someone – who's had nothing till then and then becomes financially stable – doesn't just enjoy what she has earned and simply appreciate the life that she is now able to lead. People like Ethel never seem happy with the amount they have and always want more and more. It's such a shame.

Ethel became a bit of a Hitler as she got older. For example, if you were late arriving for your shift, she would fine you ten quid for every thirty minutes that you'd missed. And she would fine you five pounds for every towel that you left behind in a room. She would never let you go home early under any circumstances; you had to finish your shift and that was that. If you were busy and seeing lots of customers, she would turn a blind eye to anything else you might be doing, like drugs or bareback. But if you weren't busy, she could be really horrible to you. I saw Ethel do things like fine girls who had only seen two customers during their shift, meaning that at the end of it they left the building having earned only ten pounds to take home with them. She would also let the guys come as many times as they wanted, which meant that they could pound the fuck out of you for an hour and come five or six times, and you would only get paid forty quid for this.

Her rules were that if a customer booked you, you had to have sex with him whether you liked him or not. I thought all these beliefs were wrong, so I used my loaf and did what I saw as tricks of the trade to get round all of Ethel's more ridiculous directives. Ethel thought that even if a guy came in and booked you, you should do him no matter how dirty he was. She expected you to service him even if he stank and had the cheesiest dick ever; because, if you didn't, you were losing her money and when she wasn't making money, she wasn't happy. Personally, I think every guy that came in should have been made to shower. But Ethel's rules meant that showers were optional for the customers.

I remember that I once went into a room with a guy, only to find that he stank to high heaven. When I got between his legs I saw that he had the thickest rim of cheese behind his balls that absolutely reeked. So I put a condom on his dick, even though Ethel expected us to perform oral without one if the customer asked. In the end I just gave him a slow wank and, thankfully, he came, so that was the end of that. After that I vowed to myself that I would never again be in such a situation and I soon found a way round dealing with customers that I didn't like, with Ethel never realising what I was up to.

First, I bought some false teeth from the joke shop. They were expensive back then, they cost me nearly thirty pounds, but they were the most real looking, ugly teeth that I could find. When I wore them, they changed my whole face and made me look awful. I would sit in the reception area waiting for the customers to come in, with my back to the receptionist so that she couldn't see what I was doing. If I knew that the guy who came in was a stinker, or if I didn't like the look of him, I would put my teeth in and smile at him and say hello – all while I was sure the receptionist wasn't looking. The guy would always look away embarrassed and never book me! Those teeth were fantastic, they worked an absolute treat. They were definitely one of my best investments.

After that, it was very rare that I copped for a stinky customer. I remember one day I forgot to bring my false teeth to work with me. I was sitting in the back room with the other girls thinking: *Shit, what am I going to do if a smelly one comes in?* At that moment, I clocked one of the girls taking her hair extensions out. She was leaving them on the side shelf in the room. They were matted, thick, black straggly things. *Perfect*, I thought with a grin. I went over and tucked some of the extensions into my knickers so that they were sticking out either side of the crotch.

Then I went to sit in the reception area. If a customer came in that night that I didn't like the look of, I would open my legs and expose Bob Marley popping out of my knickers, then smile and say hello. I found all this hilarious as the customers would look at my crotch with disgust, then look away. Those ones never picked me. The hair extensions worked a treat until about four in the morning when a piss head came in. I looked at him and thought: *Here we go, I can't be arsed with a drunk tonight.* So I opened my legs and flashed him my crotch. But, lo and behold, his face only went and lit up. I learned later that he loved hairy fannies; the hairier the better. *For fuck's sake*, I thought. *What the hell am I going to do now?* Because if he liked hairy fannies he was certainly going to be disappointed with mine, because underneath the hair extensions it was as bald as a coot. I knew that the minute I took my knickers off, my Bob Marley bush would come away too. This was false advertising and a right dilemma. I had to think fast. I looked at the customer and saw that he was blind drunk, which was a bonus.

"Do you fancy a drink?" I said to him, my brain working overtime.

"Oh yes definitely," he said with a grin. "What have you got?"

"The finest champagne," I said with a wink. "And it's only fifty quid a bottle. Why don't you buy one? Then we can get really drunk and dirty together."

The bloke couldn't get his fifty quid out of his wallet fast enough. I grabbed a bottle and two glasses off Maggie, the night receptionist, and walked into the Gold Room with the guy – Mike – in tow. I was aware that he'd booked me for an hour and was looking forward to getting started with my big hairy bush. *Jesus*, I thought, looking into his eager, drunken eyes. *How on earth am I going to blag this one?*

Mike started staggering all over the room, whilst taking each item of his clothing off and flinging it in the air. *Shit*, I thought. *I'm going to have to act fast.*

"Let's have a drink first," I said to him, jangling the glasses.

"Let me feel your lovely hairy pussy first," he said, wobbling towards me.

"Okay, but only through my knickers for now," I said with a giggle. I let him stroke the crotch of my panties for a while, while my thoughts whirred into action about my next step.

"Wow, that's a fine muff you've got," he said, slurring the words into my ear. "I can't wait to get my tongue on that."

I cringed inwardly, wondering how the hell I was going to deal with this situation. In the end, looking back, I think I coped with it rather well. I managed to get Mike to calm down a bit and sit on the bed with me. We ended up drinking the champers and chatting away. I made sure to top up his glass as soon as it was half empty, while I pretended to drink mine. I soon found out that he was actually a really lovely guy.

He was from Scotland originally but had settled in Manchester because of his work. He owned several mini-buses and had lots of contracts with the council that involved using his buses to take local children to school every day. He had been married but was divorced now and had ended up wandering into *The Edwardian* looking for company. He looked like he was in his fifties and was quite plump and short, with dark brown hair that was parted down the centre. He had a very red complexion, which I put down to the amount of alcohol he drank.

Mike ended up drinking pretty much the whole bottle of champagne by himself. As his eyelids drooped and he lay back on the bed, I began stroking his forehead. Soon, he'd fallen into a deep sleep. I lay down on the bed myself, thinking: *Thank God for that! He's not clocked my bald fanny!*

Just before the hour that he'd paid for was up, I did something that I'm not proud of. In my defence, back then all the girls did this – although I'm not saying that that makes it right. While he was snoring, I took Mike's bank card off the bedside table and crept out of the room with it. I gave the receptionist who was on that night – Maggie – his card, and told her that my customer wanted to pay for another two hours. She swiped the card and gave me a piece of paper from the machine. I picked up a pen from the desk, and went back into the room where Mike was sleeping. I signed the paper by forging his signature, then took it back to Maggie. I then returned to the Gold Room and fell asleep next to Mike.

When I woke up about an hour and a half later, I looked over at the slumbering body next to me and thought: *Shit, he's still here*. I then climbed between his legs and started sucking his cock to wake him up. Mike soon got really aroused, and his dick became rock hard. By then he was lying on his back, half awake, just gazing at me. I then proceeded to masturbate his cock all over my lips, which he absolutely loved.

"Wow," I kept saying. "I've had an amazing time with you tonight, Mike."

Bless him, he was oblivious to the fact that he'd just paid for what was basically a three hour sleep, but he was very happy that he'd just spunked all over my face. He couldn't thank me enough for our night together.

After that, Mike became a really good regular of mine. He would book me for an hour or two during most of the shifts that I worked. The second time we met, he saw that my fanny was actually bald. I just blagged my way out of having to tell him the truth, by explaining to him that I'd had to shave all the hair off to avoid catching crabs, as not all the other customers were as clean as him. He just nodded and seemed to accept what I was saying, and he never found out that I'd never had a big bushy Bob Marley fanny on the night that he'd first come into *The Edwardian*.

I also pulled another, different stunt back then, which I found absolutely hilarious. Our boss, Ethel, would never ever let any of the girls leave *The Edwardian* early. We all had to stay to the very end of our shifts. If a customer booked you five minutes before you were due to leave and go home, you had to stay and do him for an hour. This could be a nightmare if it happened at the end of a night shift. Nobody wants to stay on and work for an extra hour at seven in the morning, no matter how quiet or busy they've been that night.

I'd been working an extra shift on a Saturday night. Ethel had asked me to cover it as she was short staffed, but if truth be told I really couldn't be bothered with it. I was tired as I'd already worked the Friday night shift the day previously, and I'd spent all of that Saturday dreading going into work as I was absolutely exhausted. I'd been wondering how I could get away from *The Edwardian* early that day and all of a sudden a brilliant brain wave came to me. I walked down to the butcher's shop at the end of my road and bought a small bag of liver. I put it into my work bag and then off I went to *The Edwardian*.

I left my work bag on the floor of the girls' changing room near the radiator. I remember coming back into the room and finding the whole place stinking because the heat from the radiator had warmed up the liver and made it smell disgusting. The girls kept coming into the changing room asking me what the awful stench was and I just acted like I didn't have a clue.

It got to about two or three in the morning. I'd been busy with work since I'd got there and I'd made a fair bit of money. So I decided it was time for me to go home early, as I'd had enough of working that night. I walked into the changing room, took the liver out of my bag and went into the girls' toilet. I smeared all the blood from the bag down my inner thighs and held the clump of liver – which was dripping with blood – in my hand.

"Maggie, Maggie," I shouted to the receptionist. I made sure that the tone of my voice sounded like I was in agony. I soon heard her footsteps reaching the other side of the toilet door.

"Are you all right, Nicole?" She said.

I swung the door open and embarked on some even better acting than I showed some of the men in the parlour rooms.

"No I'm not all right," I said with a sob. "I'm bleeding really heavily, and this has just come out of me, Maggie." I held up the lump of liver in my hand. She looked at it, her eyes getting wider, as the blood from it dripped down my arm. Then her gaze went to my thighs, which were also covered in blood.

"Nicole! What the fucking hell?" She screamed, her hands going to her mouth. "You need to get to the hospital right now. Are you going to be okay to drive yourself there?"

"I feel so horrible," I said, my voice a croak. "I think you're right, Maggie. I better go and get myself seen to. I'll be okay to drive myself there."

"I'll sort out your money now," Maggie said, her face now as white as a ghost's. "And then you can get yourself straight to A and E." She turned and bustled away.

I jumped straight into the shower and washed all the blood off me. I was laughing on the inside; I couldn't believe I was actually getting away with it!

When I walked back into reception, I was acting all drowsy, like I wasn't really with it. I collected my money from Maggie, left the building, jumped in my car and drove straight home. As I climbed into my bed and pulled the covers up to my chin, I was feeling quite proud of myself. I'd beaten the system; I'd actually managed to leave *The Edwardian* early without getting told off by Ethel. This wasn't a feat that many girls ever managed.

Looking back, I can't believe what stunts we all had to pull off, just to get by, back then. Somehow, I always managed to get away with what I needed to. You just had to be one step ahead all the time, or Ethel would walk all over you. Years later, I told Ethel all about the stunts I pulled back then and she just laughed. We joke about them whenever I see her now.

Chapter Seven
Old is Gold

I soon sussed out that the older customers are a lot easier in the rooms and I began using this to my advantage by booking as many as I could. They don't have it in them to pound you for hours on end in hundreds of positions and they treat you with more respect. Nine times out of ten, the pensioners just come in for a bit of companionship, and to find somebody to cuddle and talk to. They also tend to stick with the same girl, so it's easy to end up with an older person as a regular customer who basically pays you to make them feel special and wanted.

I ended up with a load of pensioners on my day shifts, who would book me up for hours. This type of arrangement suited me down to the ground; I wasn't getting burnt out by their demands and the money was guaranteed to come rolling in on every shift. The receptionist would say to me: "Nicole, I really don't know how you cope with all these geriatrics!" I would nod and laugh, but in my head I would be thinking: *I know how I cope with them; they're guaranteed money and they're not physically draining.*

There were two oldies who would book me up every shift for hours on end. One was Brian – and we called him Blind

Brian because he only had partial sight in one eye. He was in his late seventies, very well groomed, and always wore a suit, cap and rain coat. He was slim, with a long, thin face and white, tidy short hair. He also had the cleanest, most well-manicured nails that I'd ever seen on a man. He was a doddle to deal with in the room. He had the same routine that he liked to keep to each time. We would both be naked, he would massage my back while I lay face down on the bed, then he would turn me over and start licking my pussy (he didn't have a clue what he was doing down there, bless him).

He would continue licking my thighs and pussy lips, thinking that he was turning me on. I would squeal with delight every now and then so that Brian thought that I was really loving what he was doing. On one occasion, when I was thrusting my body up and down as he was licking me, his false teeth fell out. He began feeling all over the bed, trying to find them. I decided to help him look and eventually located them under my bum. I passed them back to him, acting like it didn't bother me in the slightest. Looking back, I can see that I actually felt mortified at the time; false teeth stuck up my arse crack, what next?!

After licking me out I would literally give him a two minute suck, then he would put a condom on and fuck me in missionary. He would always come really quickly and he never wanted to experiment with any other positions. After that, we would just lie on the bed together for hours, just talking. Brian loved to listen to all my stories about my different customers. He told me that he'd been married to his wife since they were both in their teens, but that she'd recently passed away. They'd never had any children, so he didn't have any family that could look after him. He was a retired piano teacher and said he tended to listen to a lot of music to pass the time at home. He couldn't watch TV because he could hardly see anything, so all Brian had in his life was music and the hours that he spent with me at *The Edwardian* every week.

In the end, we grew quite close and he became a true friend; I could tell him anything and everything. But gradually, he became a bit jealous if I started mentioning the name of another customer too often. He didn't like me getting friendly with anyone else. Every year on Christmas Day, I would get up and make Brian and another customer Christmas dinner, then go round to their houses with it, taking some presents for them too. I didn't like to think of them spending the festive season all alone, with nothing to open or to look forward to. Brian always loved me doing this, and it made me feel happy to know that he'd had some sort of fun and love on Christmas Day.

The other old aged pensioner who was a regular of mine was called Cowboy Dave. Well, that's what we called him, anyway. And the reason for this was that he always wore a cowboy hat and boots when he came in. He was literally obsessed with cowboys. Dave was quite a character; he had a lot of mental health issues and had been in and out of psychiatric hospitals most of his life. He was around sixty years old when I first met him. He had a slim build, a freckly face and a bald head. He'd never had a girlfriend, and had lost his virginity at *The Edwardian* when he was in his late forties. He was a very good customer to the parlour and had been coming every week for years before I ever met him. He'd spent thousands in there and Ethel absolutely loved him because of this.

I'll never forget the first time that I met Dave. When I'd arrived at work that day, I'd found that the receptionist had already booked Dave into a room for an hour. I put my bag down in the changing room, got myself ready, then walked into the room to greet my customer. But at first, I couldn't see him. He wasn't on the bed, yet his clothes were. *Hmm*, I thought. *Where on earth has he gone?* I looked to my left and saw that he wasn't in the shower. It was at that point that I noticed an upside down pair of legs leaning against the wall. I walked round the bed and saw that my customer – Dave – was doing a headstand, completely naked.

"Are you okay?" I said, not knowing what else to say at that point.

"I'm fine," he said. "Doing this is very good for your circulation. You should try it some time."

"Maybe another time," I said. "Probably not today."

I couldn't believe what I was seeing; I'd never had another customer act like this before. Dave stayed in his upside down position for forty minutes, chatting away to me while I sat on the end of the bed. Then all of a sudden, he dropped his legs and said: "Right. I've had enough now. Let's go."

I was gobsmacked. I hadn't even taken my knickers off during the booking, yet I was going to be paid for talking for forty five minutes. I didn't think that Dave was going to book me again as we hadn't done anything together that day, but he ended up booking me every week after that for hours on end. Sometimes he would do his headstands and other times we would have sex. On some occasions, we would just talk. He soon became obsessed with me and started referring to me as his girlfriend. He would buy me all sorts of gifts; one day, he came in with eight pairs of shoes for me. Another week he gave me jewellery, then clothes, flowers, chocolates, money and even ornaments for my house.

One time, Dave came in to *The Edwardian* and said that if I went to his house to have sex with him, he would pay me ten thousand pounds. Basically, he wanted me to act like I was his girlfriend. Let me ask you: which prostitute would decline that offer? I certainly wouldn't. I remember thinking at the time: *Is this too good to be true? This can't be right. What's the catch?* Anyway, I took the gamble as the thought of earning an easy ten grand got the better of me. Off I went to his house and found that it was a shabby council one in Oldham. He took me upstairs and we had sex on his bed in doggy style. Then he gave me a black zip-up type folder that had ten bundles of money in it; all wraps of one thousand pounds. I couldn't believe my luck. Ten grand for shagging somebody! I really loved my job that day.

The Joy of Giving

When I got home, I found myself in a bit of a dilemma: I had no idea what to do with all my new rolls of money. I didn't need to spend it on anything as I was earning a good wage at *The Edwardian* and had already bought all the material comforts that I wanted. I actually ended up giving away all the money to my friends and family members who had absolutely nothing. I reckoned that they needed it more than I did. That's one thing I've always loved about my job; it allows me to be flush enough to buy the people I love nice gifts and to help them out financially when they're in a bad spot.

When I was a child, I remember that my Nana would always say how much she'd love to own a Royal Doulton ornament. The one she had her eye on was a big balloon lady and every time we went into Kendals – a shop in Manchester – she would look through the glass door of the cabinet at it, then sigh and shake her head, as she knew she'd never be able to afford to buy it. One Christmas, when I was earning a good wage through my work as a prostitute, I bought her the ornament as a surprise. I wrapped it up nicely and gave it to her on Christmas Day. I will always remember the look on her face when she tore away the paper and held the ornament in her hands for the first time. She was absolutely over the moon and her happiness brought a tear to my eye. This was exactly the side of my job that I loved the most: being able to afford to treat the people around me and buy them things that they wouldn't ordinarily be able to get for themselves.

I would take my son shopping for clothes and I enjoyed seeing his face light up when I was able to afford the brands that he wanted. And I loved the fact that I was able to get him what was on his wish list on his birthdays and at Christmas time, instead of having to fob him off with a story about Santa not having any of the items he wanted in stock at the minute – like I used to have to do when I was broke, before I started working. I got so much pleasure out of sending my Mum beautiful, expensive bouquets of flowers every week. I knew she loved receiving them and would array them around her home proudly.

I knew what it was like to not be able to afford a pint of milk and a loaf of bread; I'd been in that situation before. So I really appreciated the fact that now I was working, I was able to go into a supermarket and fill up my trolley without having to worry about whether I'd be able to afford all the food once I got to the till. I will never forget what it was like when I couldn't afford the flea spray and had to nick it from Boots. Or, when I wasn't able to buy any furniture for my new, empty house. Living through those experiences has given me a life-long appreciation of the material comforts that I can now afford for myself and for those who I love. When you've had money worries in the past, it's a big thing when they finally go. I always vowed to myself that I would never again go back to being that person who only owned one item in the world; a flea ridden, second hand bed. And to this day – touch wood – I've never returned to that state. And I'm so grateful for that. Because when you hit rock bottom, you get to take a good, long look at life, decide where you want to get to, and how you're going to achieve your goals. Then it's up to you – and only you – to make it happen.

Chapter Eight
Unique Encounter

Another thing that I've always loved about my job, is the variety of quirky customers that come through the doors. You never know who you're going to meet next. One of my most memorable was Alfie: the only dwarf in Manchester.

I first met him one Saturday morning, when the other girls and I were all sitting in the reception area at *The Edwardian* talking to Hailey, our receptionist at the time. It had been a steady morning and we had already done a few punters each. We were in the middle of a conversation about a new bar that had just opened up down the street, when the intercom made a bleeping noise. Hailey leaned over to look at the video camera to see which customer had arrived. I watched as her forehead wrinkled in confusion.

"There's no one there," she said, checking the monitor again. "Oh well, not to worry. Ethel told me last week that the buzzer has been playing up a bit. Must be that."

We thought no more about it and went back to our conversation about the bar. But then the intercom bleeped again. Hailey checked the monitor and I even got up to have a look at it with her. But there was definitely nobody there; the camera was just showing the empty space outside the reception area – the space between the front door and the door into where we all were, chatting. This charade went on for the next twenty minutes, with the buzzer going off more and more frequently, and for longer periods of time. In the end, Hailey got up from her chair and walked out from behind the desk.

"I think it's stuck, Nicole," she said to me. "Buzz me out, and I'll see if I can get it sorted." I did what she asked, and then sat in the desk chair watching the camera as Hailey went out of the door. All of a sudden, a man's voice started shouting: "Are you human?" *What the fuck is going on here?* I thought to myself.

Seconds later, Hailey walked back into the reception area. I could see that she was trying her hardest not to laugh. She tilted her head at me, as if to say: "Look behind me". I glanced over and saw a very small man stomping through the doorway behind her. He couldn't have been taller than three feet in height. And I could tell from the dwarf's red, screwed up face that he was absolutely livid.

"You locked me between the doors," he screamed at me. "Are you human?"

Standing beside me, Hailey managed to compose herself and not laugh, but I could see that it was killing her to hold it all in. I'd already realised that because the dwarf was so small, the camera hadn't picked him up and so we'd all thought that the entrance space between the two doors had been empty. It had honestly looked like no one was there. But the dwarf had been there all the time, getting more and more furious at being stuck between the outer and inner doors; thinking that we were doing this to him on purpose.

Hailey cleared her throat. "Which girl would you like to see?" she said, looking down at him.

The dwarf stopped ranting and the angry red colour receded from his cheeks. He stared at all four of us girls, looking each of us up and down. I'd now moved away from the desk chair and was sitting back with the other three girls on the green sofa near the desk. As his gaze swept over us, I could sense the others turning their heads away. But I kept staring straight at him in surprise. All I could think was: *I wonder if he has a normal sized penis?* Then the dwarf pointed at me and asked me to stand up. His stare took in my thigh high, black, platform-heeled PVC boots.

"Are you human?" He said to me. "Yes. Are you?" I replied.

The dwarf looked over at Hailey. "I will have her," he said, pointing towards me.

"Nicole, room one for an hour," Hailey said. "No worries," I said, leading the dwarf – who had now told Hailey that his name was Alfie - towards the staircase. I was full of anticipation at that point, wondering what size his cock would be. When we'd reached the room and closed the door behind us, I said: "Strip off."

So he did, then he got in the shower. I sat on the bed watching, completely fascinated. His dick was a normal size, it certainly wasn't dwarfed.

When he was washed and dried, I told him to lie on the bed, then started giving him a massage. He had a very hairy body and tiny legs. His feet turned out to be the same size as mine – a six. After the massage, I flipped him over and proceeded to suck his limp cock, and within minutes I'd got it hard. I could tell from the surprised look on his face that Alfie had probably never had a blow job before.

"I want to stick it in," he said, looking at me.

"Okay," I said, then leaned over to get a condom out of my bag. I rolled it down his cock, then took all of my clothes off and went to straddle his erect dick.

"No," Alfie said. "I want to do it standing up."

"Okay," I said, wondering how this was going to turn out. I watched as he got off the bed, then stood on the floor near me, with his rock hard penis pointing in my direction. I stood in front of him and bent over, but due to the height difference, his cock couldn't reach my pussy. *What the bleeding hell am I going to do with this one?* I thought. I looked down at the floor, and at that moment a brainwave came to me as I spotted my PVC boots lying there. The heels on them were eight inches high. I leant over and picked them up.

"Here, put these on," I said. I wanted to make him feel better about this, so I blagged it, saying that being fucked by a man wearing boots was a particular fetish of mine. Alfie took them and tried to get into them, but in the end I had to hold his arms and balance him there for a minute, before bending over and doing the zips up. It was hilarious, the boots went right up to his balls.

I have to be honest with you, it's quite a sight seeing a naked dwarf wear your black, thigh-high PVC boots. But hey, my idea worked like a treat. Alfie was now able to bang me from behind, while standing up. He absolutely loved it and he also loved my boots. After he'd shot his load, he started walking around the room in them, looking at himself in the mirror – he looked as proud as punch.

After our first meeting, Alfie would come in and book me every week. And I always made sure that I had my boots with me when I knew I'd be seeing him. I would get a buzz from shagging Alfie, because I knew that my ex, Matt, had a phobia of dwarfs for some strange reason. If he even saw one in a shop, he would turn and leave the place immediately. I was still meeting up with Matt from time to time, although he never had any idea that I was working as a prostitute. I was very careful to hide all of that from him. If we were together and I saw Matt getting freaked out because he'd spotted a dwarf, I would just smile to myself and think: *I fuck one of them every week and you haven't got a clue about it. And I get paid for it.* I know this sounds a bit warped, but that's just how it was.

Even though I'd packed up and moved away from Liverpool because of Matt's behaviour towards me, we'd continued with an on-again, off-again relationship for a while afterwards. He would come down and stay in my house in Manchester every now and then, but I always made sure to hide all my working gear whenever he was around. He would have been so angry if he'd ever known I'd been working as a prostitute at the same time as seeing him. This double-life style meant that sometimes I had to be quite inventive so that he didn't find out what I was up to.

Of Caning & Camouflage

Caravan Mark – as we used to call him – used to pay us ten pound per stroke of his cane. So when he booked me and put a thousand pound on the bed to entice me to have as many strokes as I could, I thought *happy days, I'll get that grand no problem, I'm going to take the lot.* So I bent over the end of the bed upstairs in Room Two and he pulled my knickers down, then he gave me ten strokes with the cane but then I literally couldn't take any more after that. He gave me a hundred pound. I looked at my arse and it was black and blue. Matt was coming down that day, and I knew he'd suss that something was up if he saw the bruises all over my bum. I thought: *How can I blag this now?* So I came up with a plan and when Matt arrived in Manchester I took him to a park that night and fucked him all over the place, standing up against different trees, and making sure that my arse was banging off every one of them. The next day, I turned over and showed him my bruised and purple bum cheeks. "Oh baby," I said, looking up at him. "Look what you did to my ass last night!" *Phew*, I thought, as Matt bent over to look at the bruises on me, convinced he'd caused them. *Got away with that one!*

Also, at the end of every shift at *The Edwardian* I would have a wee and then not wipe myself so that I wouldn't smell too clean for Matt. I usually had showers after each client but I knew that he would suss that something was up if I came home smelling of scented soap each time I saw him. I was careful like that.

A Near Death & Other Experiences

Alfie the dwarf was by no means the only quirky customer who I had at *The Edwardian*. One of my regulars was a producer from a popular TV soap. I will always remember what happened during my friend Hailey's first shift on reception. This producer – who used the name Gary – had booked me for several hours in The Fantasy Room that day. Basically, I knew that he wanted me to tie him up and shove a dildo up his arse, and then drug him up with poppers. So off I went downstairs to the big red room in the basement to meet him.

I tied him up, put the dildo up his arse and turned it on, and then I crawled to the top of the bed to give him the poppers. But after a while, I thought: *Gary's not really getting high on this*, so I tipped the whole bottle of poppers on to a tissue, put the tissue on his head, and then put three pillows on top of his head to hold the tissue down. My thinking was that this way, he'd get a really big hit. Now, bear in mind that Ethel – the boss – only bought the most expensive duck-down pillows; they were dead heavy, a bit like bolsters. At the time,

I thought Gary would be all right with this amount of weight on him, I just thought it would help him to get really high. But the next thing I know, his all-year-round tan drained from his body in an instant, the grey paleness starting with his ankles and then going all the way up his skin as far as I could see. Then he let out a massive croak, and in a second he was as dead as a doornail.

I immediately left the room and ran up the stairs screaming: "I've killed him! I've killed him!" There's a buzzer system in *The Edwardian*, and I started shouting at Hailey:

"Let me out the back door right now!"

I was crying my eyes out at this point, because all I could think of was the headline that would be in the *News of the World* the next morning, (the trashy paper that liked doing sensational exposes still existed back in those days). I could imagine my son finding out that his mum was a prostitute from this bloody paper. I'd kept my work separate from Scot up till then and had no plans on telling him where I earned my money. I was trying to pull my jeans on all the while I was talking, I just desperately wanted to get away from the place and go home. I kept thinking: *Oh my God, I'm going to get locked up for this. I've just killed Gary.* I was panicking so much.

Hailey and the other receptionist who was on – Tracy – went running down the stairs to the basement. "Nicole," Tracy shouted up a few seconds later. "Get down here now." So downstairs I went, crying my eyes out because I knew that this producer Gary was lying deceased on the bed. "You could have fucking untied him," Tracy yelled as I walked back into The Fantasy Room. She was busy undoing all my knots, with Hailey by her side helping her.

A few minutes later Hailey had gone back upstairs and rung for an ambulance and, to be fair, it turned up pretty quickly. The paramedics did CPR on Gary's lifeless body straight away. And, fortunately, the producer let out another massive croak a few seconds after they'd started and came back to life! Meanwhile, I was still in hysterics in the corner of the room. I remember how the ambulance crew tried their hardest to convince Gary to let them take him to hospital to get checked over, but he absolutely refused. Probably because he didn't want his wife or family to know where he'd been, or how he'd got injured. So the paramedics made him sign a form that proved that he was refusing to go with them. That was one hell of an intense day. Hailey – who is still one of my closest friends all these years on – and I talk about the incident now and laugh. But at the time, it wasn't funny at all.

Then there was an old man who used to come into *The Edwardian* and book me; he used to make me wear his dead wife's clothes. She'd been a Charleston Dancer and he would ask me to dress up in her lacy old dresses that had tassels swinging off them. He was about ninety and he would just lie on the bed masturbating while I was going round the room singing "Charleston, Charleston." He would bring in his music from the olden days to complete his experience and I'd have to dance round the bed to it for an hour while he had a wank. He was pretty nuts.

Another guy who booked me from time to time was basically a torso, he had arms but no legs and he would come in wearing a nappy. His back was all bent, bless him. The only way he could get around was in an electric wheelchair. I remember watching him climb on to the bed while I lay there. His arms were really strong, which isn't surprising really- they were all he had to get about with. This guy would book me just so he could worship my feet and legs for hours on end. He would kiss and lick me from my thighs to my feet, and then suck each toe individually. It must have been his fetish because he didn't have any of his own. You meet some heart-wrenching cases in brothels too; people who literally have nowhere else to go to get their needs met.

A Sassy Show & Subterfuge

One hilarious thing that happened at *The Edwardian*, was when a TV producer called Stan turned up one day and told us that he was making a documentary about UK brothels with a man called George McCoy, who writes about UK massage parlours. Stan asked us if anyone would be up for appearing in the show and told us that if we did we'd be paid fifty pound a minute. Now me being a dickhead and thinking of the money, agreed straight away.

But I'd temporarily forgotten that my husband Matt – who I was still having an on-off relationship with – still didn't know that I worked in a parlour. It wasn't long before the whole TV crew had arrived, together with the writer, George McCoy, and they were filming me as I lounged about in a Jacuzzi. They had me drinking champagne and drooling over the writer George McCoy. We all then went downstairs to the Fantasy room in the basement, where there's a pole fitted, and it wasn't long before I was twirling round the pole in my thigh high PVC boots, thinking I was someone out of Pretty Woman. George was seated in an armchair near me, watching, saying to the camera: "Oh yes. You can even get a lap dance in here."

So after that, I was buzzing because I'd earned an easy few hundred quid. Then I suddenly thought: *Shit! Matt's going to see me on TV when this airs! He'll recognise my fat arse swinging around anywhere!* The production crew had informed me that the documentary was going to be shown on TV round about Christmas time. For weeks all I could think about was what would happen if Matt and I were sitting there watching the telly one night, with Matt deciding to flick over to a show about British brothels, and all of a sudden hearing my gob, and seeing me sitting in the Jacuzzi in *The Edwardian*, with George McCoy in his flat cap watching me and drooling away. I mean, it would be quite a sight for Matt to behold, as a girl called Christine had been sitting next to me, and we'd both had our tits out, making provocative and sexy noises, like "Oh yes, George" and "Ooh". George McCoy was loving it, like he was Hugh Hefner in the Playboy Mansion or something, staring at our bare breasts while they bobbed around in the water. He was saying things like: "You can even have a glass of champagne in the Jacuzzi after you've had a good shag."

If Matt saw me, even wearing a mask, he would surely recognise me. And he would literally kill me. Or, if he didn't recognise me in the Jacuzzi with my tits out, he would one hundred percent recognise my huge fat arse jiggling around the pole in the Fantasy Room. If I'm honest, the whole situation was really stressing me out. *How could I be so stupid?* I kept thinking.

Then, I had a brainwave. It came to me suddenly and in one second I knew how to stop Matt ever seeing George McCoy's documentary. I went round the house, taking every fuse out of each of the plugs. This way, none of the televisions in the house would work. The good thing was that Matt wasn't very clued up when it came to electrics, so I knew he wouldn't bother trying to fix the situation. The end result was that we didn't have a single TV to watch over the whole, entire Christmas period. This suited me down to the ground, as I was more than happy to just listen to music.

But as Sod's Law would have it, George McCoy's documentary didn't end up getting shown over the Christmas period in the end. In fact it didn't air until several months later, the following year. By the time it was shown, Matt and I had broken up for good so it was no longer a problem, and to this day I still have no idea whether he ended up watching it. It's mad to think back and realise how petrified I was of him seeing it. Nowadays – years later – I couldn't give a shit. But when you're in an abusive relationship, the fear you have for the man you're with is totally unimaginable. However, years later, when you're no longer with that person, you look back and wonder why you were so bothered. It's mad how things change, including our opinions of people, as life moves on.

Back then, Matt scared me more than anything. I remember bumping into him years after we'd separated, and I felt absolutely no fear whatsoever. I look back now, and think to myself: *Why did I put up with him for so long?* I can't answer that question. I only wish that I'd left Matt sooner. When you're in an abusive relationship, you can't really see what's going on, when you're in the middle of it. You can only see the situation for what it was once you let go and look back at it. Sounds crazy, but it's true.

Loads of soap stars who lived in Manchester used to come in to see us girls when I worked at *The Edwardian*, although, if they were recognised too much by the people who worked there, they would get the hump and leave. Some of them were raging coke heads. I've shagged some famous footballers too. Funnily enough the people with the most money – like the footballers - would often book the cheapest room. Well known politicians would come in to the parlour sometimes too and you would never believe the MPs – and cabinet ministers - who I've fucked! Particularly the ones who've done work for Manchester, but I can't really say who. Lots of police used to come in; I think the boss would pay them backhanders so they would leave us alone and not raid the parlour. *The Edwardian* is officially a 'massage parlour', because working in a brothel isn't legal in the UK. Sometimes parlours do get raided, but if they're not causing any trouble, the police often leave them alone. There are occasions when the emergency services have to get involved with brothels; drugs are probably the most common causes of deaths in brothels; there was a death in one in Manchester just last week. A customer overdosed and that was that. And events can get a bit dicey when customers want to be covered in black bin bags to the point where they can hardly breathe, but I'll talk more about that later on in the book. The next parlour that I went to after *The Edwardian* is where customers' tastes got even freakier...

Chapter Nine
Luke, The Gift Horse

To be honest, working at *The Edwardian* felt like one big party. But the beginning of the end of my time there started the moment that I met a rich headhunter from Leeds who came in and booked me one night. He was tall, with dark hair, probably in his late forties. It turned out that he was absolutely rolling in money and his wife owned her own dentist's practice. He was well groomed and smelt of expensive aftershave. His accent was posh Harrogate and, as a prostitute, I found it easy to smell the money on him. Sniffing out wealth is a trick of the trade. He literally had money coming out of his ears. He'd booked the Fantasy Room in the basement and when we got down there turned to me and said: "I'll book you all night and give you an extra five hundred pounds if you do gear with me." "Gear?" I said. "I don't take that stuff." I thought he was talking about heroin, because to me that's what 'gear' meant. Everyone I knew called it that. But it turns out that posh people call coke 'gear'.

The man – who we'll call Luke – cut up a tiny line of cocaine on the bedside table. I looked at it; I'd never taken the stuff before. I didn't know how it would make me feel.

"Will it kill me?" I said, turning towards him.

"No," Luke said, smiling. "It's completely safe. You'll feel great, I promise."

Well, I thought to myself. *I've taken speed in the past and I was all right with that; that stuff there looks just like whizz. And if I snort it he'll give me five hundred quid and book me all night too. I'll try it.* So I had a tiny line of it and found that it made me feel a bit like I did when I was on speed. It perked me up and made me feel awake and happy. I quite enjoyed it, to be honest.

I ended up snorting coke all night with Luke and doing all the degrading things he asked me to do to him, like spitting on him, calling him a worthless piece of shit, strangling him, kicking him in the balls, and pinching his nipples. It was mild dom, a lot of verbal. Luke wanted me to get into his head like that; it's what floated his boat – he couldn't get enough of it. Domination isn't just screaming your head off at somebody, although a lot of people think that's all it involves. In reality, it's more about giving someone a head fuck. If you can get into their brain and get them to believe what you're saying, you've nailed it. It's a mind game. And in actual fact, this feels more intense to the customer than just repeatedly hitting them. The smaller and more belittled they feel, the better. And it was clear that Luke liked what I was doing to him; I must have got it right.

After that session, he began to book me on a regular basis. Every Friday, he would give me a five hundred pound tip and I ended up earning ridiculous money from him. His only two stipulations were that I snorted coke with him and dominated him all night. Easily done and I was happy to oblige. After a couple of weeks, he was booking me from the minute I went into *The Edwardian* to the second that I went home. He was already a drug addict and it now seemed like he was becoming addicted to me.

After this arrangement had been going on for several months, with me dominating him on many a night, Luke turned up at the brothel one day and said to me:

"Nicole, I want you to be my mistress. I'll give you an allowance and you'll see only me – no other customers – twice a week. I'll buy you a house wherever you want and obviously you won't have to work in the parlour any more." I thought: *Fucking hell, this is like pretty woman. I can't believe it. Is this really happening?*

And then he said:

"I don't want to see you in here, I want to see you in a hotel instead, until we get your house sorted. And I'll give you two and a half grand a day, plus the five hundred pound tip for being a good girl."

No contest, I didn't even have to think about this offer. I was up for this deal. It was stupid money that he was offering and there was no way that I was going to turn this kind of gift horse down. So we started seeing each other every week in the Crowne Plaza in Leeds. I'd meet him in the hotel at about ten or eleven o'clock in the morning and I was done and home by six in the evening. Luke would have a pile of cocaine ready and waiting on the coffee table in the room each time I got there. It was honestly like the film Scarface, when Tony Montana is sitting there with a white mountain in front of him on the table. We'd drink loads of bottles of Bollinger too and I would basically dominate him all day. So far so good, everything was working out nicely and I was more flush than I'd ever been.

By that point, Luke knew where I lived. He'd promised me all these things, like a new house and car – although they hadn't actually materialised yet. He'd told me a bit about himself too, that he was married with twins and had originally come from Harrogate. As I mentioned before, his wife owned her own dentist practice. He said that he owned his own headhunting company, but, looking back, I'm sure that there was more to it than that. No one has the amount of cash that he does by running that sort of company; if you ask me, I think he could have been high up in the drugs world. Somewhere in the upper echelons of the spectrum; he was so well spoken and nicely dressed that there was no way he'd be just a lowly drugs mule. Definitely not with the Porsches that he owned. The amount of cocaine that he always had ready and waiting was insane; he obviously had easy access to the stuff. I didn't question this too much at the time, but, looking back, it's difficult to believe that he was just the owner of a company and nothing more. Mainly because - most notably - he was literally dripping with surplus cash all of the time. Maybe the head hunting business was just a legitimate façade to explain away his millions? Who knows.

I had no feelings for Luke whatsoever, it wasn't like we were forming some sort of meaningful romantic relationship during the time that we were seeing each other. The only thing that I was arsed about was his money, to be quite honest with you. I wasn't sexually attracted to him, it was purely domination. And in my experience, you can't fall for someone who you're dominating anyway, because there's no intimacy there. It's role play. It's far removed from the type of 'normal' sex people usually have in a relationship. It could get quite hard core but we always had a password, which was Cinderella. So if I was going too hard on him, he would say "Cinderella" and then we would stop and have a break or a line of coke.

Then, one particular day, Luke was already off his head when I met up with him. I knew that something was different as soon as I walked through the hotel room door; I could just sense that he wasn't right. When you work as a prostitute, you learn to analyse people very quickly. It's a skill that keeps you safe. Nowadays, I can walk into a room and sum up everyone in there pretty quickly, because you learn how to use your gut instinct. And I've learnt to always follow mine. On this particular day, I started off dominating Luke like usual, doing things like pissing on him, getting him to lick my arse and things like that. Then, when we'd stopped for a bit, he turned to me and said: "Can I dominate you for a change?"

This request freaked my head out a bit, but I thought: *Fuck it, I've got two and a half grand in my bag already as also a five hundred pound tip and this guy says he's going to buy me a house in whatever area I want.* So I agreed to let him dominate me and Luke immediately sat on my face and went into role play mode. But what he was doing didn't feel right to me. Now, bearing in mind that I was off my head on coke at this point, awful headlines started running through my head, like: *Prostitute Found Dead in Leeds Hotel Due to Suffocation by the Balls.* I remember him pushing his balls on my face while he was looking down at me and I couldn't breathe. I was thinking: *Fucking hell, this is weird.* At the time I just acted all blasé like it was fine but, in my head, I was freaking out.

Luke was getting more and more weird as the day went on and then the final straw was when he said that he wanted to put a plastic bag over my head and suffocate me until I was at the point of near death. I'd never done that to him, and warning bells started going off in my brain as soon as he suggested it. I thought: *Hang on a minute, this isn't right.* And he'd been going on and on all day about this place in London – although I'm not sure how true this is – where women go and let men dominate them. Basically, he said that the girls there earn thousands at a time, because blokes pay them loads of money to do serious damage to them, like breaking their noses or arms. In reality, they torture the girls there and the workers have to have months off work to recover, but lots of them think it's worth it because they get paid so much money. If I'm honest, I wouldn't be at all surprised if a place like that probably does exist. There's something for everyone these days. And Luke said he was really keen to take me there. Looking back, if I'd been willing for him to start hurting me, he would probably have ended up doing some serious damage to my body, or even killing me – given what he was clearly into.

When I looked up, Luke was holding a plastic bag in his hand. I thought fast, and managed to get out of it by saying that I'd only just realised what the time was and that I had to get home. Thank God, my excuses worked and I left the hotel immediately. I remember how dark the night was at the time and how scary it was walking down to the car park on my own. I had a white Fiesta at that point, which Cowboy Dave had given to me. Bear in mind, I was off my head on coke and I was paranoid now that Luke was about to come up behind me holding the plastic bag. I realised that day that there was another side to Luke that I hadn't seen before and I didn't like it one bit. I managed to get into my car without anything horrible happening and I was freaking out all the way to Manchester, thinking that every car that came up behind me was Luke's.

I always go to my Mum's house when I'm in distress, so it wasn't long before I pulled up outside hers, coked off my head with my heart going a hundred beats a minute. I put my key in the door, turned it and walked in. My Mum came out into the hall. "Oh hello Nicola," she said. "Have you got your Avon money?" Up until this point, I'd kept my working life a secret from my Mum. But that night I was so upset, I just came out with it and told her the truth. I pulled all these thousands of pounds out of my bag, and said:

"Listen, forget the Avon money, I've got something to tell you. I've been in a hotel all day, dominating a guy. He's paid me all this money. And I also work in a massage parlour in Manchester. It's really posh," I said quickly, as I watched her face crumple. "It's great there, Mum, it's got marble Jacuzzis. It's not what you think."

By now my Mum was full on crying. "I can't believe it," she said between sobs. I went and wrapped my arms around her. "You're no different from those street girls, Nicola." But after she'd calmed down and we'd chatted some more, she turned to me and said: "Listen. I won't accept your job, but I'd rather live with it and keep you, rather than make a fuss about it and lose you. I don't agree with it, but no matter what, you're my daughter."

Looking back, telling my Mum about my job was the best thing I ever did. Because after that, whenever I knew Matt was coming down to Manchester to see me, I could hide all my work gear at hers because I knew that he would literally kill me if he found out that I had sex with other men for money. I would stash my PVC boots and working clothes at hers and Matt never did find out what I was up to back then. Anything that I bought with my earnings, I would explain away to Matt by saying that my Mum had bought it for me. I told him that she'd bought me my new big TV and my black leather two and a half grand couches and he believed me. My Mum wasn't thrilled about this, but it worked a treat. In the end, Mum came to kind of accept what I did for a living, although I can't say that she was ever all that happy about it.

After that horrible experience with Luke, I left *The Edwardian* and went to work at a brothel called *The Pelican* instead. Luke had freaked my head out so much that I decided that I never wanted to see him again. Money is power and he had so much of it that I knew he could have me dead if he wanted. I'd never experienced anything like that before and I knew that I definitely didn't want to go through something similar again. That's why I left. However, I did go back to *The Edwardian* just once a few months later and worked one shift, but, as luck would have it, Luke came in that night and looked me straight in the eye while I was sitting in the reception area. My heart rate sped up as I stared back at him. He'd spent that much money in there that Ethel had let him have a tab and he'd come in to tell the receptionist that he wanted to pay it all off. And that was the last time that I ever saw him, thank God.

No one apart from Luke and his mate – Coke head Tony – was ever given a tab while I was at *The Edwardian*. But they had so much free cash that Ethel made an exception for them. Sometimes Coke head Tony would book into *The Edwardian* for a week and just move into the Fantasy Room downstairs. He'd have a continuous stream of girls sent down to him and happily paid eighty quid an hour for their services. And then, when he got bored of the girls, he'd just pay to sleep in the room. It was crazy, Luke and he had silly money. And the problem with that is that sometimes those people with silly money can start doing really stupid things. After I'd seen Luke holding that plastic bag in his hands, I knew that I was totally done with him and I had to leave *The Edwardian* so that he no longer knew where I was. So I got myself a job at another parlour, *The Pelican*. And that's when things started to get really crazy...

Chapter Ten
Fetishes & Peccadilloes at The Pelican

I'd heard about this brothel called *The Pelican* through word of mouth. I was too scared of Luke to go back to *The Edwardian*. I knew that I needed a new place to work in and was looking around for ideas. I also had a day job by the time I switched parlours; I'd started working for a sales and marketing company called Caldwell Communications in Manchester. I found out that the shifts at *The Pelican* would suit me down to the ground, because the timings of them meant that I could still go home and have enough sleep to get up in time for my day job. The shifts there were either from midday to six in the evening, or from then until midnight. And when you've got a nine to five office job, those kind of hours fit perfectly around it.

I was nervous about working anywhere else and I'd heard that the owner and madam of *The Pelican* was quite picky, so I wasn't sure if she'd take me on. She was called Vera – in fact she's written her own book about her life as a prostitute and madam. But I made an appointment to see her anyway and drove to Swinton where *The Pelican* was, hoping that the meeting would go well. I walked into the building – which was directly facing a pub – and up the stairs and found that the parlour was located in a flat directly above a video shop.

After I was buzzed in, I saw that *The Pelican* was nothing like *The Edwardian*. There were three dingy rooms for the girls to work in, with single beds in each, a little tiny dungeon sort of place, and the reception was a small area with a desk and a corner couch. That was pretty much it. It wasn't at all what I'd been expecting; I suppose I thought that it would be more glamorous and well kitted-out like *The Edwardian*. It smelt like a pub in there, I remember. There was loud Reggae music blasting out and it was full of cigarette smoke.

I ended up getting on really well with Vera and she decided that she would take me on to work there. She was a right character. She was very well spoken and she'd initially worked as a prostitute before she'd become a madam. Vera had had a lot of work done to her body: she had tits like Lola Ferrari – the biggest implants she could get - very full pouty lips like a puffer fish and long, blonde hair extensions. She was probably in her sixties when I first met her. She wore velour tracksuits and crop tops, and because of her privately educated background and elocution lessons, she spoke dead posh.

Vera was nice to me and we seemed to get on well, so I accepted the job and started working for her that night. Another girl and I were there working in two separate rooms, which smelt of sex, sweaty bodies, breath and condoms. And during the six hour shift I found that I could do twelve customers back to back. Plus, I'd get extra for doing oral without a condom – which Ethel at *The Edwardian* didn't allow us to have – so I got an extra ten pound per customer.

The maths are simple: if you do oral without a condom on twelve customers it's an extra one hundred and twenty pound; and if you do it to completion it's an extra two hundred and forty quid. And on top of my income for twelve customers, that's good money. So even though *The Pelican* was smaller than *The Edwardian* and wasn't done up as nicely when I first started there, I quickly ended up earning more money than I had at my previous parlour. And also, I was doing inbound retentions for Caldwell Communications as my day job, and getting eight pound a retention there plus my basic and the commission. So, I was probably getting three or four grand a month from my office job. I had a lot of money coming in but I spent as I earned back in those days. I wanted designer everything and I was driving an eighteen thousand pound car at the time. But you live and learn about spending and saving the hard way sometimes, don't you?

I liked Vera a lot. She wasn't afraid of having attitude. If someone called in that she didn't take a fancy to, she was a bitch to them. And if a girl turned up for an interview and Vera didn't like the look of her, she'd say: "Oh Darling, you're not a Pelican girl. There's the door." And the girl would have to turn around and leave the building.

That was Vera all over, that was the way she spoke to people; drawling her vowels and sounding super upper class. I found out that she was an only child and had had a nice, privileged upbringing, but had then rebelled and started working as a stripper, then a prostitute and, finally, a madam. After her book *Eating from the Cherry Tree* came out, she was interviewed on the chat show *This Morning*. And in true Vera style, she put her hand down her top at one point, drew out her business card that had her number on, and gave it to the presenters! She could be a bitch but I liked her and she was all right with me. I enjoyed becoming part of her team of girls. At the start of every shift, Vera always smelt of soap powder and strong, flowery perfume. As the shift went on, she would start smelling of strong wine. She really loved to drink wine! I remember how she always had a look of Joan Collins about her, although back then her hair was blonde. She had fantastic legs and was an ex-ballet dancer; a fact that showed in her posture.

A lot of the customers at *The Pelican* wanted straight sex and oral, but there were also several freaky fuckers, each of whom had their own particular fetishes. I used to work with a woman there called Fay, a blonde Scouser who I loved. She was probably in her fifties back then, so she was my Mum's age. To be honest, Fay taught me everything I know. I'd never done half of the things that I went on to do at *The Pelican* before I started working there and it was Fay who helped me get confident with all the new stuff.

One day it was me and her working a shift and she ended up being my first lesbian kiss. I'd gone into the room with her and the guy who'd booked us wanted us to kiss; I was thinking: *Oh my God,* because I'd never properly snogged a woman before. We were on the bed and she started necking with me.

It actually felt normal and okay. Then she went down on me – she was very good at that – and she actually made me come. I was embarrassed because it was a woman doing it but after that I soon got used to it.

I'd done lots of two girl jobs at *The Edwardian*, but that was when two of us had sex with a guy together. At *The Pelican*, the customers wanted us to have lesbian sex together a lot of the time. I've got a high sex drive and I can come off someone licking me out quite easily, if they do it well. It's one of the perks of the job. In fact I can go into a room with a customer who I'd never look at twice on the street and find that the sex is absolutely mind-blowing and intense, because I've just clicked with them sexually – never mind how hanging they actually look. I've had ninety year old men make me come before. You never know what's going to happen until you get into a room with that customer.

I got more and more open minded the longer I worked at *The Pelican*. I remember a guy that came in who was nicknamed Mr Smith by the other staff, a name I didn't understand at first. He always used to book Fay, but one particular day - when I was wearing a nurses outfit - he came in, looked at me, and said, "I'll have Nicole today." Fay looked over at me when he said this. She wasn't smiling. I can remember her next words exactly as if she'd said them yesterday: "He's having you today. If your favourite meal is steak and chips, then that will always be your favourite meal. But now and again you'll go off and have a bit of egg and chips. But you'll always come back to your steak and chips."

She was basically saying that she was the steak and I was the egg, and after having me he'd come back to her! Just bitchy, but that's how women are. She was just jealous that he'd booked me that day and not her. So Mr Smith and I went off to the room and I noticed that he was bringing a carrier bag with him. If you see a customer with a bag, that's when you know that things are going to get freaky. It's a dead giveaway. When they come in with a bag, you can guarantee that something weird is about to happen. So anyway, I then went out of the room, allowing Mr Smith some time to get undressed and washed and all that. Then when I returned I saw that he'd laid three apples out on the side of the bed. I looked at them, thinking: *Right, what's going to happen here then?* I watched as Mr Smith positioned a waterproof sheet under himself on the bed. I spotted a flannel that he'd placed next to the apples, as well as a big can of air freshener.

I soon discovered that Mr Smith wanted me to put the apples up his arse. He lay back on the bed with his legs in the air and he talked me through how I should put each apple near his arse hole then pop it up there with the can of air freshener. I had to push them up one by one until all three were up there. And then I had to go to the top of the bed and rub his head with the flannel, and say: "Come on, push, push," like I was a midwife. "I can see the head, its coming. It's a boy!"

So he would push these apples out of his arse, like he was giving birth. And I would stand there telling him he was having a boy or a girl, or whatever he wanted to hear. And I realised that that's why they called him Mr Smith at *The Pelican*, after the apple brand Granny Smith, because he was so obsessed with these bloody apples! I went over the top with it because he loved this whole process. I would rub his hair and say:

"Slow down, I can see you're having another contraction." I just elaborated as you do, improvising as we went along. I was in acting mode.

Mr Smith liked me, and took a bit of a shine to me after our first encounter, ending up booking me every shift. I got used to seeing his arsehole dilate as I pushed the apples up it, opening up until it looked like a big rabbit hole. Then one day, he came in very excited. "Nicole, Nicole," he said. "Come here, I've got something different for you today." I thought: *Oh for fucks sake, what's he brought in with him now?*

So as usual I put him in the room, then went out so that he'd have some time to get ready. When I went back in, I saw that he'd lined three pears up on the bed instead of apples. I thought: *Blimey, he's really pushing the boat out today. Happy days.* So after he'd got himself all ready on the waterproof sheet, I pushed the first pear up his arse and it went up a treat. The second went up nicely too. I couldn't get the third up because it had a nobbly bit on the end. Then Mr Smith started pushing, and one of the pears popped out. But he couldn't get the other pear out of his arse. It was stuck up there and nothing seemed to budge it. He was doing the pushing and the panting and I was mopping his head with the flannel; we were changing the way he had his legs, I had him on all fours, then standing up, but that pear just wouldn't come out of his arse. I couldn't finish the service and he had to go to hospital to have the pear removed.

I didn't see Mr Smith for a few weeks after that and when he did come back in to the brothel he'd gone off using the fruit; he'd clearly had enough of it after the pear incident. Instead, he told me that he'd had another idea. When I went into the room to see him that day, I found that he'd laid out loads of syringes on the bed. Then he asked me to bring in the bin from another room. I noticed that the syringes didn't have the needles in them, he'd only brought the barrels in with him. He asked me to go through the bin and take out all the used condoms, then suck the spunk up from each of them with the syringes, then inject all this spunk up his arse. He asked me to tell him that I was injecting him with AIDS while I was doing this. All the while he was masturbating on the bed. Looking back at all this I can see that he was a freak, honestly.

Another time when Mr Smith came in, he wanted me to pretend that I was his sister and that our Mum was watching us have sex. He wanted me to leave the door of the room open and was telling me that he was going to get me pregnant and all this stuff. He was very strange indeed. One time, when we were chatting, he told me how he used to go to the gay sauna, and how he was put in a chair, so that all the gay men there could go through him. He said he really liked them doing this. When I looked at his face, I could see that he wasn't the full shilling. His eyes said everything.

There was another guy who used to come into *The Pelican*, who we called Graham the Dog. To be honest, he freaked my head out the first time he booked me, because I'd never seen anyone wearing the full gimp outfit before I did his booking. He'd arranged for us to be in the tiny dungeon room, which had a small electric chair type of thing in it. It looked like the death penalty chair, although obviously it wasn't, it just had straps on it. When I opened the door and saw him in there for the first time with his gimp mask on – black rubber that covered his face with just a hole for the mouth - it was quite shocking and scary.

He'd brought a bowl with dog food in it with him and he wanted me to feed him the dog food through the mask, so that he could eat it. So that's what I did. Another time, he wanted me to go through all the bins – like Mr Smith had asked me to do - and take out all the used condoms, and then tip all the spunk out of them and into his mouth. I remember watching as he drank it all. Then I had to put the last condom in his mouth put my hands over his lips, and make him chew it. Later on, when I'd left *The Pelican*, Graham the Dog actually became a tranny. People who were into certain fetishes really found their niche at that parlour.

Sex was dead open at *The Pelican*. If a customer wanted to shag you in the reception area while other men sat there waiting to book in, then that's what you did. You'd do your booking in front of everybody. So say if someone had booked me for half an hour and there was ten guys sitting there in reception watching the porno that was on the telly, I'd have to go and suck the guy's dick in front of everyone if that's what he wanted. And also fuck him in front of everybody, if he was up for it. To be honest, doing this did make me more open sexually. Everyone else watching us would now have that twitch and urge from what they'd just seen, so the job was half done with them before they even got into the rooms. They were nearly ready to explode. Or, sometimes, I ended up doing a couple of guys at once in reception, sucking them both off at the same time. It's just how it was there.

I remember how these two guys arrived in the reception area at the same time once; they were both business men and clearly didn't know each other from Adam. I went into the room with both of them and at that point I'd never been in a room on my own with two guys. As it happened, they kept looking at each other and I was analysing their body language; I could tell that they were attracted to each other. They ended up giving each other sixty-niners on the bed, these two married men, sucking each other off, and then I actually got one to penetrate the other. It was great, I got paid for the booking with these two guys, without actually having to physically do anything myself.

One day, a husband and wife came into *The Pelican*. I thought: *Oh for God's sake, I've only ever kissed one other woman – Fay – and she's licked my fanny, and I've gone down on her. Looks like I might be having another girl tonight though…* I could immediately tell that the wife didn't want to be there. Her husband was a big fat man with a pony tail and he was definitely the dominant one in that relationship. The wife was very shabby and mumsy and was wearing an anorak. A long, dark skirt was sticking out from under her coat. Underneath that she had bear legs and was wearing Doc Martin boots. She looked very poorly maintained and had straggly hair; you could just tell that she had a shit life. I could see immediately that her husband was a twat and was the boss in their house, that her life with him was basically crap. If he demanded that she cook him dinner, then she would have to, no questions asked. She didn't want to be in our parlour, but he'd blagged her to come in. I didn't like that sort of behaviour one bit.

They'd booked to see me for an hour together. He wanted to watch me go on his wife, but bear in mind, I'd never done this with any other woman apart from Fay at this stage. So I was in the room thinking: *What the bleeding hell am I going to do with this woman here?* I wasn't feeling all that confident about it. So at that point, I decided to get my friend Diane - who was working with me that night - to come in on the booking. That way I felt a bit more confident, having some friendly moral support in the room.

I said to the woman: "You're going to have to have a shower love, before I can lick your fanny." So she's in the shower and from where I was sitting on the bed I could see that she just didn't take care of herself. She had hairy legs and she was standing with her back to me; I could see the water dripping down off her pubes. She had a real Bob Marley hairy muff. Her husband was standing there all eager, ready to watch his wife do a lesbian thing with another woman. But I could see that her head was hanging down despondently, bless her, which was another sign that she just wasn't happy about what was going on.

The woman took her time in the shower, probably because she didn't want to do this lesbian thing that her husband had brought her to the brothel for. When she eventually got out, Diane was ready on the bed, and encouraged the big-bellied woman to come and lie down next to her on her back. Her husband was stood in the corner with his dick out, wanking away, obviously excited by the prospect of seeing his wife get it on with another woman. I looked over at him, and thought: *For fuck's sake*. I really didn't like the way he didn't care one bit about his wife's feelings. I looked back at the woman and wondered what to do. I nodded at Diane and she started playing with the lady's tits. I thought: *Well, it looks like it's up to me to do the deed then.* So I started kissing the woman; necking with her. And then I started going down on her, taking my time around the belly button. Eventually I got down to her big fuck-off hairy bush. But as I went to put my head near her twat: *Urgh*. I stopped. Her fanny absolutely stank of ammonia, it was proper disgusting.

Now, bear in mind that I'd just watched this woman have a shower and she still smelt like this after washing herself. I thought: *What the fuck?* But I had to style it out because her husband was watching and wanking away in the corner. And, also, I was well aware that the poor woman didn't even want to be in *The Pelican* in the first place. I was in acting mode and I didn't want to upset anyone; but there was no way I could put my face near her pussy again. I knew I had to get on with the show and couldn't let my real feelings about the smell be at all obvious. So I decided to spit on my finger and rubbed her clit instead. Then a little while later, she shuddered while she was lying there on the bed and her legs did a twitch, as though she was coming. I knew she hadn't really come and that she was just playing the game for her husband – who was clearly getting kicks out of watching all this.

"Did you come then, love?" Her husband said loudly, from his place in the corner. "Ooh yeah," the woman replied. But I knew she hadn't really, I'd hardly done anything to her at that stage. So the man was all happy, thinking: *My wife's just come because of another woman.* I looked at him, and thought: *You're a cunt, you. Your wife did not want to come in here, she didn't want to go with another woman. I don't like that kind of behaviour. And you're not going to get away with it that easily. Right, you fucker...*

"You get on the bed now," I said to the man, reaching over and getting a bullet – a small vibrator – off the side shelf. "Lie faced down, that's it." Diane and I got on the bed and started massaging him, then I started playing with the bullet round his arse hole. After a while, I began slowly prodding the bullet in to him and the next thing I know, the suction from his arse has sucked the vibrator right up inside. It completely disappeared up his bum hole! I was thinking: *This is karma, this.* I couldn't get it out and I didn't want to stick my finger right up there as I didn't have a condom on it. His wife was laughing and elbowing me, thinking that this new development in the proceedings was great. She knew that I knew that she didn't want to be there, so now we were kind of in cahoots against him in all this.

Well – to cut a long story short - we couldn't get the bullet out, so the man had to go home with a vibrator up his arse. He was absolutely fuming. But his wife was happy, as she'd never wanted to come in the first place. That couple never came in to *The Pelican* again, thank God, which I was glad about as I didn't like how the man had made his wife do something that she clearly wasn't comfortable with.

So life at my new brothel went on like this for a while, with me seeing lots of clients and earning a good income. But then a couple of years after I started working there, Vera bought the video shop downstairs, and had the whole parlour made over. It was really nice after that, she spent thousands on it. When she was finished, there was a big open bar downstairs, all red with LED lights and a nice carpet. She also re-did all the rooms upstairs and themed them; one was a fantasy room with different uniforms, she did more work on the dungeon and created a sexy third room. The result was modern, trendy and plush, more like a club. And that's when Vera decided to start hosting sex parties at *The Pelican*...

Chapter Eleven
Surprise Customer

I remember one incident that happened at the brothel before Vera started holding the parties. I was still working my day job at the time at Caldwell Communications. Vera left a message on my phone saying that someone had read a great review about me on the internet and was pleased to hear that I was very good at sucking cock, and had decided to pre-book me. I didn't know who it was, but I thought: *Happy days*, and after I'd finished in the office I made my way to *The Pelican*, ready to meet my new customer. As it happened, the traffic was really bad that evening and I got stuck in several jams, meaning that I was a few minutes late for work. My customer had already arrived and booked himself in when I got there, so I put my bag down, got myself ready, and put my hooker gear on; ready and raring to blow! So, off I went to the room, opened the door, and saw a guy lying on the bed faced down. Then he turned round to acknowledge me and I smiled back. It was at that moment that I realised that the man on the bed was the guy who sat opposite me in the office at Caldwell Communications. A shocked look washed over his face.

"I-I-I've only come in for a massage," he stammered, checking out my outfit. "I didn't know this was a brothel, I thought it was just a massage parlour. What are you doing here dressed like that?" He was looking genuinely embarrassed and I knew that this hadn't been a calculated move on his part; he hadn't known that I worked at *The Pelican* before he'd arrived and seen me in the room. I thought: *Fuck that, you lying bastard. You knew perfectly well this was a brothel, you just didn't know that I worked here.*

So, I made damn sure I sucked his dick and fucked him that night, I made damn sure he came, and I never went back to work at Caldwell Communications after that. I couldn't go back, because I knew this bloke was a right gossiper, and now that he knew I worked as a prostitute at *The Pelican* in the evenings, he would be sure to spread rumours about me all over the office. After I left Caldwell, I concentrated on working solely at the parlour.

Partying at The Pelican

Shortly after that, Vera started holding her sex parties. *The Pelican* was now the perfect place for them, what with the more upmarket makeover, and the big bar that was now downstairs. The parties were really good. About twenty odd blokes would turn up and eight girls would be working; it would basically turn into one big orgy. Vera would put a buffet on too and it wouldn't be unusual to see a guy eating a cocktail sausage while having his dick sucked at the same time. I found the parties really fun. We'd get paid about two hundred and fifty quid each for two hours and we'd have a laugh and make the most of it.

However, I can clearly remember one particular day when Vera was holding a party and there should have been eight girls working, but only four of us turned up. The problem with this was that Vera let twenty eight blokes in. Now, with the best will in the world, there is no way that four girls can do twenty eight blokes in two hours. It's physically impossible. That party was horrendous, the men wanted sex and if they could have shagged our noses or ears, then they would have done that. After a while, I was physically fucked, it was exhausting trying to service so many of them by ourselves. We were getting banged out left, right and centre, spit roasted, it was just horrible. You'd be sucking a dick and have another one poking you in the eye at the same time. It was overwhelming. All Vera was thinking about that day was her pocket, she didn't give a crap about us girls or what we were having to do. When you do an orgy, you should do a maximum ratio of three to one. Four girls to twenty eight blokes was ridiculous; it was impossible.

Another girl – Portia – and I ended up on the bed together in one of the rooms. All I could see around us were a sea of cocks. There were so many men there, hungry for sex. I thought: *What the fuck can we do here?* Basically, I started necking with Portia, then going down on her, telling the guys that we wanted them to spunk all over us. There was about forty five minutes of the party left at that point and my plan worked a treat, the guys masturbated and then came all over us while we were going with each other on the bed. But one of them squirted spunk into my eye and I couldn't see after that, it hurt so much it was really horrible.

No matter what I did, I couldn't get it out, and my eye went bright red and swelled up. I was shaking because I hadn't eaten and I'd been doing such a lot of physical activity for over two hours that my body was fucked. Someone gave me an eye bath, so I plugged that on my eye, went downstairs to the bar, and started eating an egg mayonnaise butty off the buffet. My hands were trembling so much I couldn't even get the sandwich in my mouth. It was at that point that Vera walked in. She stared at me.

"What are you doing in here?" she said, obviously not happy that I wasn't off shagging one of her twenty eight party guests. "I've got spunk in my eye," I said, removing the eye bath so she could see the redness and swelling. "Oh, you'll be all right," Vera said breezily. "Go back upstairs and do some more work." It was the little things like that which I didn't like about her. All about money and no compassion if you were hurt.

So, back I went upstairs for a while and then as the party was finishing, all the blokes, the girls and I, came back down to the bar. There was all the buffet food still sitting on the side, hardly touched. To finish off the last few minutes, Fay decided to put some cocktail sausages up my fanny, because she knew that I can fire things out of it at will. It was a good way to end the entertainment, as I was so fucked and hungry by then I don't think I could have physically done anything else. I felt like a one eyed prostitute at that stage, as my eye was still killing me and I could barely see out of it. As I fired food out of my fanny, Fay ate it, and all the men wanked over us, and that was the end of that particular party. Vera liked us to work up to the absolute deadline and then she would cut it off.

After the men had gone home, the other girls started complaining to me about the working conditions that night – as they knew I have a big gob and am not afraid to speak my mind. "Nicole, we should be getting more money than two hundred and fifty quid, for what we've done tonight," they said. "We've had to work so much harder because the other girls didn't turn up. The pot should have gone eight ways not four to begin with, but seeing as half the girls didn't turn up we should be getting their share too, for servicing all the men by ourselves. Can you go and say something to Vera about it?"

So I went over to the boss and asked her if I could have a word. "Yes darling?" She said, turning her head towards me. I explained to her about how the four of us had had to work a lot harder than usual that night, what with the other girls not showing up. Twenty eight blokes had come in, which meant that earnings would be well up – I knew she could afford to pay us more - and I said that the other girls and I would appreciate it if she gave us more money than just the two hundred and fifty quid, seeing as what we'd done for her business that evening.

Vera then gave me the dirtiest look ever, like I'd just shat in her mouth or something. Then she walked off and had a think about what I'd just said, with her head held high in the air, clearly not happy about it all. And then she turned and walked back towards me. "I'm not happy about this, you know," she drawled in her posh accent. "But I've decided that you can have another fifty pound each for tonight." That kind of Scrooge-like behaviour was just Vera all over. Like with Ethel – the boss of *The Edwardian* – she had an element of greed about her. It's sad, but it's just how these madams can get.

The girls at *The Pelican* were a nice bunch and I made good friends with them. Apart from Fay, there were Portia, Chanelle and some others. As I said earlier in the book, I've never met a prostitute who hasn't been through some sort of domestic violence in her past and it was no different with the girls at this parlour. We used to go out and have drinks together outside work, and laugh about what we'd all been getting up to at *The Pelican*.

I little while after I started working there, I met a barrister, who came in and booked me one day. My relationship with Matt had completely finished by then and the barrister – John - and I got on well, and, eventually, we started seeing each other outside work. As time went on I developed feelings for John and, for a while, everything was hunky-dory. We had good times together; we travelled all over the country and stayed in nice hotels. And I would sometimes stay with him in his apartment in Manchester City Centre. But the downside - as I discovered – was that John could be a bit pompous. I actually got pregnant by him, but then his well-to-do family said that I'd only done it to get up in society. So I ended up having an abortion. It is what it is. And then we separated. Shortly after that, I met the man who would become my daughter's Dad at a friend's barbecue. He was lovely and we ended up getting married.

Nicola Harper

Quirky Customers & Random Ruminations

Meanwhile, the stream of quirky customers kept coming to *The Pelican*. I remember a judge called Roger who used to come in and get off his head on coke. He used to do all the parlours and he would literally take any drug that you'd give him, so I used to sell him pro-plus – the energy tablets – and tell him that they were ecstasy. He was already snorting coke so he was none the wiser and after he'd taken it I would go a bit daft with him in the room, and say: "Wow, that was amazing Roger. Fucking hell that sex was good!" But really I was just trying that bit harder, because I was getting fifteen pound a pro-plus from him, when they'd only cost me two quid for a packet.

Another time, I didn't have any coke to sell to the judge, but I did have some speed which I'd got off somebody at work. It's much cheaper than cocaine, but I thought: *I know, I'll sell it to him at coke price, he'll never be able to tell the difference.* So a few seconds later, Roger the judge was bent over the side table snorting whizz! He soon got off his nut because you can't really snort speed like you do with coke; it got to the point where he was gurning away and could barely get his words out. It was so funny. He was all right, Roger, he was just a raging wreck head. Then he'd go into court the next day and do his job, like he hadn't just spent the previous night getting fucked in a brothel. Crazy times.

Then there was a customer called Dave who got in with the wrong working girls. I remember how, to start with, he used to own his own company; he had loads of money and drove a Jaguar. He used to come into *The Pelican* for hours and have a good time. But then he started sniffing coke with some of the girls. At one point we didn't see him for months, but when he did come back in it was clear that he'd progressed from coke to crack cocaine. He wasn't driving his flash Jag any more, he arrived that time in a clapped out old banger. His smart clothes had turned shabby and to pay for his half an hour he pulled out a bunch of crumpled up five pound notes, which seemed very different from the flashy credit cards he used to use. He'd lost the plot; I remember how he started pointing to a tissue on the floor thinking it was a rabbit. It was sad to see him fall from being a successful business man to being milked dry by a working girl who was a heavy drug user. He went from being addicted to coke and then, on to crack; my guess is that he's probably so far gone now that he doesn't even own a car. He's lost everything. It's sad, that. But we all have our own choices to make in life, don't we?

Chapter Twelve
'Fuck a Book'

We had our fair share of quirky customers who came into The Pelican. One of them was a little Chinese man who came in and booked me one evening. He was tiny – only about five feet tall – and painfully thin. His face looked so much older than the condition of his body. My guess is that he was probably aged around forty at the time. He had spiky, jet black hair and bad skin. I had previously heard about a guy who the other girls at the parlour had named 'Fuck a Book', but up until that point I'd never had the pleasure of meeting him.

After this guy had booked me, we went into a room together, and I remember how I started massaging his tiny body on the bed. Then I took all my clothes off and proceeded to rub my bare nipples up and down his back, while gently stroking his balls from behind to try and get him aroused. Usually – with most customers – this gets them going and hard pretty quickly, so that when you flip them over, their dick is already erect. Confident of this usual outcome, I asked him to change position from lying on his front, to lying on his back.

At that point I saw that he had the smallest, limpest penis I have ever seen. (In my experience, Chinese people tend to have really small cocks with pubes that – in my opinion – look like cat hair; thick, dark and straight.) But this guy's dick seemed abnormally small, probably about the size of my thumb fingernail. *How the fuck am I going to suck that?* I thought to myself. *Oh well, it is what it is.* I climbed in between his legs, parted all his cat hair like pubes, and tried to give him a blow job. But it just wouldn't work. All I was copping for was a load of pubes up my nose. As the Chinese guy stared down at me, I remember thinking: *I bet he thinks that I look like I've got one of the Chuckle Brothers' moustaches right now.* The whole situation wasn't even remotely sexy and I was wondering what the hell I could do to move it forwards.

Then I had a bright idea. *What if I start fingering myself for him?* I thought. *Maybe he will get off on that.* So, I lay back on the bed trying to be all sexy, then parted my legs and started rubbing my clit (which was probably bigger than his penis). I then proceeded to shove my fingers into my pussy, while making my best groaning actress noises. The man looked at me with confusion and shock on his face.

"What are you doing?" he asked.

"Masturbating," I replied.

He looked at me again.

"No," he said, his tone very abrupt.

I watched, startled, as he then leant over the side of the bed, and then did something very strange. He pulled out a child's story book from underneath his pants on the floor and passed it to me. *What the fuck?* I thought, turning the book over in my hands. *This man wants me to read him a kid's story half way through a session?* I opened the book and looked at the first page. There were pictures everywhere and not much writing. The book seemed very used. I looked at it again, then I looked up at him. "There's not much to read in here, Hun," I said. "I think you might need to buy a new one, some of the pages are stuck together."

The man then leaned forwards and snatched the book off me, and proceeded to do one of the strangest things I've ever seen in my life. He put the book on the floor, then lay on top of it, and with the book open underneath him, he rubbed himself up and down on it, like he was fucking it. It didn't take long before he gave a massive grunt and ejaculated all over the pages.

Meanwhile, I was sitting on the bed watching all this with my mouth wide open, not knowing what to say. After he'd come, the man didn't acknowledge me at all. He just stood up, got himself dressed, bent down and grabbed his jizzy book - clutching it to himself like it was worth its weight in gold - and then exited the room. Looking back, I've never understood the method with that man, '*Fuck a Book*', and I don't think I ever will. It was all so strange to watch. '*Fuck a Book*' still does the parlour circuit now, all these years later. To be honest, I'm not sure if he's still using the same book, or if he's updated it to a new one. So bizarre!

BEHIND THE BUZZER

Nightmarish Anecdote

I had spoken earlier about Fay, the glamorous blonde Scouse lady with the most amazing pair of long legs at *The Pelican*. As far as I am aware, she will be in her sixties and still works; she can pull in the boys even now. When it was quiet in *The Pelican*, Fay would tell me stories about the most bizarre customers that she's serviced during her working years. I will never forget one particular customer that she told me about. His name was Bill. She said he would come every Wednesday into the parlour that she was working in and have an appointment with her at exactly 2.30 pm. Bill would always arrive half an hour early for his appointment and would sit there in the reception area, wearing his smart suit, tie and shiny black shoes.

Fay said that Bill was probably in his fifties back then and that he liked to have a cup of tea and read the newspaper, to relax before each booking. He was always polite and would make small talk with Fay and the receptionist. When he had finished his cup of tea, Bill would go up to the room at exactly 2.30 pm; he always liked to be very prompt about everything. Then he would have his shower and lie on the bed face down, waiting for Fay to come back into the room. When she walked back in, Fay told me that she would strip off completely naked, and then give Bill a slow and erotic massage, rubbing her bare breasts up and down his back, kissing his neck, then slowly licking down his spine. When she got to his bum, she would lick his balls from behind, slowly teasing him. Then she would turn him over on to his back and start slowly licking up and down the sides of his cock, still carrying the teasing on. When Bill was almost ready to blow his load, she would grab a condom, rubber him up, and then get on all fours and wait for Bill to mount her from behind. He would then stick his stiff cock in her pussy and fuck her until he shot his load.

I remember Fay saying that she had suggested to Bill that he might like to try some different sexual positions but that he'd politely declined. He only ever wanted to go through with that same routine. I've found that a few guys are like that, to be fair; they want the same thing every time that they visit and they don't like change.

So at that point, Bill never seemed any different from any other punter to Fay. Six months down the line, he came in as usual for his weekly Wednesday appointment one day and I remember Fay saying that nothing seemed out of the ordinary with him. She didn't suspect at all that things were about to turn horrible. Bill went through his usual motions, having his cup of tea and reading his newspaper in the reception area, before arriving at the room at 2.30 pm exactly, to have his shower.

Fay walked into the room when he'd finished getting ready and started off on her normal routine with him. She gave him his erotic ball-teasing massage, flipped him over, and started licking his erect cock. Then when he was nearly ready to blow his load, she put a condom on him and got on all fours ready for him to fuck her from behind. But then suddenly her gut instinct told her that something wasn't right. She put her hand beneath her to feel his cock and felt something sharp on her finger.

"What the fuck?" She screamed, jumping off the bed and turning round to see what it was that she'd just felt. It turned out that Bill the Cunt had made a leather pouch that went over his cock and put six inch nails all through it, so that it was covered in sharp spikes. He had every intention of shoving this horrific invention up Fay's fanny. At that point, Fay said that she went nuts. Melting into a hysterical mess, she smacked him, and then ran downstairs screaming. When she heard what had happened, the receptionist promptly ran upstairs and went crazy at Bill. He got dressed very quickly and then Fay and the receptionist dragged him down the stairs and kicked him out of the building. Bill was never seen in the brothel again after that.

What a sick cunt, he must have calculated and planned for months for that to happen. He'd intentionally built up Fay's trust over a period of time, just so that one day he would get the chance to seriously hurt her like that. Imagine if she hadn't followed her gut instinct and felt behind her; the whole incident could have ended in tragedy. Bill would have penetrated her with a load of nails covering his dick, and would have probably ripped her insides out. Hearing stories like that one make me feel that this is why parlours are a safer place for prostitutes to work in, rather than by themselves in their own houses. If that had happened to an escort who was alone in their own house

– or in someone else's – things would have ended disastrously. What a cunt!

Compulsive Customer

I've had my own weird – sometimes unpleasant - experiences with customers too. There was the time when I was working in *The Pelican* one evening, when a short, fat, grey haired old man came in. He was wearing glasses and struck me as a bit odd as soon as I looked at him. There was just Fay and I working that night and I remember how the receptionist – Julie – called us both through to meet this man after he'd arrived. The guy peered at us both through his spectacles and then said in a slow voice: "I will have Nicole for half an hour." So I escorted him up the stairs to the room, asking him what his name was on the way. "David," he said, in a quiet voice.

I asked him if he wanted to have a shower but he declined, so I left him in the room to get ready and went back downstairs. When I went up and into the room again, David was lying on the bed on his back, stark naked. He had a huge belly like Mount Everest, that had a massive lump on it near his belly button. The lump was so large that he couldn't lie faced down on the bed because of it.

I started chatting with him and it turned out that the lump on his stomach was a hernia. David said that he'd visited *The Pelican* a few other times and booked different girls, but that this was his first time with me. He said that during his previous visits, he'd only ever had a wank. I knew straight away that David would become an easy regular of mine if I could get him to like me. I knew that he didn't have it in him to bend me into every position possible, and pound me until my back ripped. This was very appealing, because as I've mentioned elsewhere in the book, I like to have easy customers as they mean easy earnings for me. So, to keep him sweet, I decided to give him something he'd never had before: a blow job.

"I'm going to do something very special for you, David," I said. I climbed between his legs and started to slowly stroke his small, limp cock. The longer I did this, the harder it got. Once it was fully erect, I spat all over the end of it, then rubbed my spit up and down his stiff prick. Then I opened my mouth – while looking him in the eye – and slowly put the tip of his cock in between my lips, letting all the spit from my mouth dribble down it. I made sure that we maintained eye contact all the time.

"Ooh Nicole, I've never done this before," David said, delight in his voice. His little stumpy legs started to shake and I could feel his cock beginning to throb on my tongue. I knew he was about to explode. I took his dick out of my mouth – which was now rock hard and dripping with my spit – and started to wank him off. All of a sudden he gave a huge grunt and started to twitch, then he ejaculated all over his huge belly. It was at that moment that David became obsessed with me. Nobody had given him that sort of attention before and he clearly absolutely loved it.

From that day on, David would book me during every shift that I worked, sometimes for hours on end. I didn't mind as he was easy in the room and once he had come he would be quite happy just lying on the bed, cuddling and talking to me. But after a while, David started getting a bit possessive, asking me if he was my favourite customer, and things like that. If he knew that other guys had also booked me, he would go into a mood. It got to the point that when I arrived at work, he would be sitting outside *The Pelican* in his red Ford Fiesta, waiting for me. I can still remember his car's registration all these years on, it must be burnt into my brain.

As time went on, David really began to freak my head out. I remember one day, I was driving down my Mum's road with my son in the car. I looked in the rear view mirror and suddenly realised that David was behind me. It wasn't possible for me to stop my car and say something to him, because I had my son with me. So I just kept going and hoped that he would go away. On another occasion, I glanced through my front room window and saw that David's car was parked right outside my house. When I went to the front door and opened it, he sped away. When he came into the parlour I would ask him about these events, but he just flat out denied that they'd happened.

The final straw came one night when I'd just finished a shift at *The Pelican*. I was dropping my friend Diane home. It was one in the morning and the roads were dead. I remember how we were driving down Washway Road in Sale, when I turned to Diane and said: "I'm sure that car behind us is following us." I'd been keeping an eye on it in my mirrors for a while. Diane turned round and looked through the back windscreen. I decided to slow right down so that the car behind us would have to get really close to us. When it was right near my bumper, I looked in my rear view mirror and immediately recognised who was driving the car: David. I was fucking furious. At that point I knew that I'd had enough of his behaviour. It had to stop, there was no way I was going to put up with someone following me around like this, it wasn't right. I slammed on my brakes, got out of the car, and walked over to him.

"What the fuck are you doing following us home, you freak?" I screamed at him. I knew that I needed to shock him, or he'd never stop stalking me. But as usual, David denied that he was following me. So I went absolutely nuts, leant through his car window and punched him in the face. This might sound extreme, but I'd got to breaking point with his stalking and nothing else was working. I was sick to death of him following me around in his bloody red Ford Fiesta. It had got to the point where he trailed me everywhere I went and his behaviour was really starting to fuck with my head. Where would it end? What other more extreme measures was he prepared to take? It had to stop and that was that. After I punched him, David revved up his car and sped away.

After that night, I refused to see David whenever he came into *The Pelican*, and it wasn't long before he moved on to another girl. I was so relieved when that happened. That's the only problem with giving customers the attention that they've never had; if you give them too much they start reading more into it than it actually means. People like David start getting possessive and convince themselves that you are actually their girlfriend. I've seen the same thing happen to other girls hundreds of times. Customers – especially the needy ones – don't understand that we are simply doing our job; we are not getting romantically involved with them. What goes on between the customer and the girl is a cash transaction for a service, nothing more. All prostitutes are actresses who are playing a game; when we are working it's like we're on stage becoming whoever that customer desires us to be. Don't get me wrong, when we orgasm it's not always false. Like I've said before, you can just click with certain customers and have amazing sex with them. But even on these occasions, it's still simply a cash transaction for a service at the end of the day, nothing more.

Chapter Thirteen
Bizarre Customers

Of course, we had many normal customers coming into *The Pelican* as well, and, by "normal", I mean your straight sex and oral kind of guy. Don't get me wrong, many of the men who came in to the parlour would fall under this category. But I've chosen to not really concentrate on these ones throughout this book, because there are plenty of other works out there that do this, and, to be honest – these men are just having the kind of regular sex with working girls that goes on in bedrooms across the world every day. It's nothing new, everybody knows about this kind of thing. These guys tend to be nice people and I've become friends with a lot of them during my years in the sex industry.

However, what I wanted to concentrate on in this book – and what you don't hear about very often – are the more bizarre customers who come into parlours. I've chosen to do this because I want the outside world to see what really goes on in the places that I've worked. Yes, there are the normal guys. But there are plenty of quirky and unusual customers who want to do things in the bedroom that you could never imagine in a million years. I have to be honest: in my world, I seem to attract the more weird and quirky customers. I think this is because I've always made a point of not acting shocked when they tell me their bizarre requests, as I don't want to make them feel uncomfortable. I never want them to feel awkward acting out their fantasies; I'm quite accepting of people in that way. So they feel like they are understood in my parlours and, in the past, have often followed me from one parlour to another when I changed my place of work.

For example, there was a guy who would frequently book me at *The Pelican* called Paul. He was really good looking – the stereotypical tall, dark and handsome type. He was probably in his early thirties back then. I have to admit that I really liked him and was also attracted to him sexually. In my opinion, Paul was pretty perfect in every way; he had a huge cock, too, so what more could you want? The first time I walked into a room with him, I actually felt really awkward because I was so conscious of how good looking he was. It was like I had a school girl crush on him. I couldn't wait to see how the booking would pan out...

When the door had closed behind us, Paul asked me to lie on the bed next to him, fully clothed, so I did exactly that. Then he asked me to show him my knickers, so I pulled up my PVC skirt and my black lace French underwear. He smiled, then lent over the side of the bed and pulled something out of his trouser pocket. I looked over, and saw two pairs of black silk full panties.

"Can you put these on instead, Nicole?" He said.

"Course," I replied, accepting the pair he was offering me before taking off my knickers and putting the ones he'd brought with him on.

"Would you mind if I wear the other pair?" He said.

I looked at him, not letting my surprise show on my face.

"No, course I don't mind," I said.

So Paul – quite proudly – put on the other pair of black, silk panties. We both just lay there on the bed together for a while. Then he reached over, pulled up my skirt and started to stroke the crotch of my panties. Then he grabbed my hand and indicated that I should do the same to him; he wanted me to stroke his crotch too. It might sound silly, but this whole rubbing of the crotches was really turning me on. I could feel myself getting wet. I was kind of hoping it would lead to more...

"Let me just grab my poppers," he said, reaching over for the bottle. When he'd had a good sniff, he said: "Put your hand down my knickers and wank me off, Nicole." So as he took another big sniff of his bottle, I reached down into his panties and began masturbating his huge prick. I could feel him starting to throb, then he exploded all over the inside of his panties. Every time Paul booked me after that, he would always want exactly the same service, which ended with him spunking into his silk knickers. *What a waste of a huge cock*, I would always think to myself after each service. In the end, I never did get to fuck Paul. But hey, panties and wanking is what turned him on, so that's what we did. And he left the parlour a very happy customer.

Then there was a huge Asian guy who would come into *The Pelican* quite often, known to us as the 'Condom Man'. I can remember how he would always arrive at the door right at the end of a shift when we were all tired and had made our money, and were just looking forward to going home. All the girls would dread him booking us, because we knew that if he did, he would ask us to go through each of the bins in the brothel and collect every single used, spunky condom. When all of them had been gathered together, the guy would ask whatever girl he'd booked to tip the jizzy contents of each condom into his mouth and then make him drink the lot. After that, the girl would have to lay him on the floor and then piss into his mouth while he wanked himself off. Trust me, when you're tired and just want to go home at the end of a shift, the last thing you want to be doing is siphoning through bins looking for used condoms for the Condom Man.

Another bizarre customer that I once met in *The Pelican* was the Balloon Guy. This man would like to go into the room, pump up a series of different coloured balloons, and then, when the girl came into see him, he would be lying on the bed naked with about fifty inflated balloons all around him. He would then ask you to grab the balloon that was the colour of his choice that day, such as red. He would then want you to say: "I'm going to pop the red balloon!" And as you did so, he would lie there all happy, wanking away, saying: "Oh Nicole, tell me again."

This process would have to be repeated with all the balloons and I would have to pop each one while Balloon Guy lay on the bed and masturbated until he came. This was hard work to be honest, as the balloons were huge and really hard to pierce. I can remember how they made such a loud noise when they exploded that it hurt my ears.

Another guy who came in to that parlour called Zed stands out in my head against all the other weird and wonderful customers. He would like to book me for half an hour, during which time he would hurl abuse at me from the moment I stepped into the bedroom to see him. He would say things like:

"You're a dirty whore, Nicole."

"You're such a dirty slag."

In return, he wanted me to beat the shit out of him and spit in his face. He really liked it if I marked his skin or bruised him. The more severe I got with him, the larger the tip he gave me at the end. I've seen Zed leaving a room with two black eyes, as happy as a pig in shit. He was one customer who sure did like to be beaten. How very bizarre!

I also remember the tax man who would come into *The Pelican* quite a lot. His name was Steve and in my opinion he looked a bit like Barry Manilow. I can remember the first time that Steve booked me as clearly as though it had happened yesterday. But then, an experience like this would be hard to forget. Basically, I turned up at work one day and as I came through the door, Julie the receptionist said: "Ah Nicole, you've got a booking with 'Jump On Your Head Steve'." I looked at her, thinking: *What the fuck*? I couldn't say anything or ask any more questions as the guy – Steve - was sitting there on the sofa, staring at me. *Oh well, fuck it, I'll just have to deal with it,* I thought, taking a deep breath.

"Would you like to come with me?" I said, smiling at the man. He stood up and I realised from the way he started lurching towards me that he was very drunk. I led him into the room, then left him there for a few minutes so he could get ready. When I walked back in a little while later, Steve was lying on the bed fully dressed, with his shirt unbuttoned.

"I can't suck your dick with those jeans on, Hun," I said. "Come on, get them off."

He looked at me, his eyes all glazed.

"I don't do that," he said.

"Well what service do you usually have in here?" I said, trying not to look surprised.

"You need to jump up and down on me with your heels on," Steve said.

I stared at him, thinking: *Oh God, what the fuck?* Then I looked at his body, and thought: *Oh well, I'm just going to have to give this a go if that's what he likes. It can't be that hard...*

I braced myself, climbed up on the bed, and proceeded to jump up and down on Steve's chest and head while wearing my heels. This might sound easy to do, but trust me, it's not. And as I learned over the next few weeks, Steve knows perfectly well that it's not an easy thing for a girl to do to him, and in his own bizarre head he gets off on watching the prostitute wobbling around and struggling to jump up and down on top of him for thirty minutes. I've seen Steve leave parlours on numerous occasions where he's been stomped black and blue, with heel marks all over him. To be quite honest with you, I don't understand what sexual kick he gets from having a girl jump up and down on his chest and head like that, but, hey, each to their own. That's 'Jump On Your Head Steve' for you. And the moral of this story is that you never know what anyone is getting up to in their private life, not even a tax man.

Cagey Casey

After I'd worked at *The Pelican* for a while, I kept hearing both girls and customers talking about a girl called Casey. I had never met her, but was becoming increasingly intrigued about who she was. I was also noticing that when I was going into the room for bookings, more and more customers were asking for bareback sex (sex without a condom). Even those who were normal married men were requesting it. And these were customers who'd never ever asked for it before, so I knew something unusual was going on in the parlour. Basically, bareback sex is normally a big 'no, no' for prostitutes for obvious reasons HIV, hepatitis and all the other sexually transmitted diseases, for starters.

Eventually, I ended up working a shift with this elusive Casey. She was a very polite black African lady. She had tiny boobs and when she wore make-up, she looked very young – about nineteen – and had a childlike figure to go with this. When she wasn't wearing any make up at all, she looked completely different, maybe aged fifty. And with make-up, she actually looked a lot prettier than she really was.

During the first night that I worked with her, I just knew something wasn't right. Every time I went in to a room that she'd previously used, there were no condoms at all in the bins. To me, this was a dead giveaway that the rumours about her doing bareback were true. Also, I clocked that she was coming out of each booking with an abnormal amount of tips. Customers usually pay more for extras, but the amount she was getting was silly. No man is ever going to give you a hundred quid tip for something small. And it wasn't like she was getting hurt by a customer, as I've previously described happening with Peter the Beater.

When I took a good look at Casey, I noticed that the whites of her eyes were yellow. At that moment, I instantly knew that this girl had hepatitis. Yellow eyes are always a dead giveaway for this. So I told Vera the boss, explaining about the bareback and the fact that Casey was most probably spreading hepatitis through the customers.

Now the thing is, Casey was financially very beneficial for Vera, because she was booked up solid and was bringing loads of money into the brothel. But the plain fact of the matter was that Casey's behaviour was putting everyone – customers and girls alike – at risk. After I'd finished explaining the situation to Vera, she put her head on one side and thought for a minute.

"I don't know whether I should follow my heart or my wallet," she said eventually. Her words made me absolutely fume. How can you risk everyone else's health just to make a few easy quid? I normally really liked Vera, but at times like this her greedy, selfish attitude really pissed me off.

Anyway, the situation eventually sorted itself out, because one night Casey ended up copping off with Vera's bloke and Vera got rid of her after that. She was absolutely mortified that her fella had been with one of the girls, especially the one who had hepatitis. Oh, how the tables were turned that day!

It turned out that Casey was actually living in a psychiatric hospital in Salford and, on certain days, she was allowed out on day-release. She would use that time to come and work at *The Pelican* and when she'd finished her shift, she would go and buy a load of crack cocaine, smoke it, then make her way back to the hospital. She was put in there, in the first place, due to having psychosis caused by her crack abuse.

The crazy thing is that I first started writing this book when I was in the exact same psychiatric hospital as Casey had been living in. I was in there because I had a breakdown, but, hey, I'll be telling you all those details much further down the line…

Chapter Fourteen
The Stereotypical Brothel: BJ's

After I met the lovely man who would go on to become my daughter's Dad at a friend's barbecue, he didn't want me working as a prostitute at *The Pelican*. So I moved on from this type of work and started working at the reception desk instead. I was happy to do this, as I didn't want to upset my boyfriend. But at the same time, I saw a big drop in my earnings when I stopped servicing the customers. This was mainly due to the fact that Vera would only give me one or two days at the desk per week, as it was a role that she liked to take on herself. She was very good on the phone and knew exactly how to sell the girls to the punters, so I could understand her reasoning behind this. After a while of working the desk at *The Pelican*, I knew that I needed to supplement my income with something else, as the bills wouldn't pay themselves and I never wanted to be in the position where I was struggling for money again.

So I got a job down the road at a brothel called *BJ's*. I was offered more money than Vera was paying me, so it was a no-brainer; I accepted the job and started working at the reception there. To start with, this was a part time position and I was still doing one or two days a week in *The Pelican*. But it wasn't long before I was offered five days a week at *BJ's* and, as this was clearly a much more lucrative and worthwhile position for me, I decided to completely leave Vera's parlour and went to work at *BJ's* full time. The hours were better at my new place of employment; we'd start at ten in the morning and finish at eight at night. Much nicer than working all through the evening and going home at midnight.

I remember parking near *BJ's* on my first day, round the back of a block of flats. I walked to the building and went up the five metal steps to the black metal door. I pressed the buzzer.

"Hello, can I help you?" A rough Mancunian voice said.

"I've come for the reception job," I said. "My name's Nicole."

"Come in," the voice replied.

The door opened and I walked in. Directly in front of me was a steep set of dark stairs. I walked up them and at the top of them was a woman – probably in her late forties – with long red hair and a petite figure; probably a size eight. She was dressed in a blue tracksuit top and trousers. I later learnt that because BJ was so tiny, she often had to buy child size clothing. She was extremely clean and smelled like she'd just got out of the bath. There was also an odour of weed about her – I later learned that she constantly smoked it. As I got to know her overtime, I realised that she was exceptionally intelligent. She put her head up to greet me.

"Hi Chicken, I'm BJ," she said. "Nice to meet you." I introduced myself and we shook hands.

"I'll show you around," she said. As we started walking, I instantly noticed how different this place was compared with *The Edwardian* and *The Pelican*. It was very dated, décor wise. The walls were half dark green and half dark red, with a dado rail separating the two colours. The floor was covered in a dark red, Axminster-type carpet, the sort that my Nana had in her house when I was a child. There were slutty pictures of naked women adorning the walls, all of them in dusty frames. Everywhere I looked, there were sex toys, dildos, butt plugs, strap-ons, whips, chains, paddles and nipple clamps, all hanging off the walls. You name it, BJ had it. Also, there were mannequins everywhere, that were dressed up in wigs and trannie uniforms. It wasn't like anywhere I'd worked in before, to be honest.

It was horrible. But then it suited what it was and a lot of customers say that they like coming to a place like that. Because they say that in a place like *BJ's*, they really feel like they're in a proper brothel. They like to have that experience, the old fashioned seediness of it all. The whole place stank of cigarettes, cigars and poppers, and filthy sweaty sex, because – as I was to learn – a lot of orgies went on in there. It also smelled of bums, because – as I found out – a lot of the guys who frequented it wanted some kind of anal play. There was also a strong aroma of Calor gas fires, because that was what BJ used to heat the place. I was to learn that they would be constantly on in the winter and that the smoke from them would make me feel drowsy.

The two rooms with the double beds in them were sinister, dark and seedy spaces. They had a sink but no shower. They had clothes rails in them with the most bizarre array of costumes I've ever seen. Gimp masks, adult baby grows, cowboy outfits, loads of PVC items, huge pairs of knickers, clown costumes, sissy dresses and gas masks from the war. They were the weirdest collections of clothes that I've seen in my life. In between the two rooms there was a middle one that was painted black; the Dungeon. A Saint Andrew's wooden cross was attached to one of the walls, with handcuffs and ankle shackles bolted on to all four corners of the cross. At the side of it, there was a shelf that had paddles, canes, riding crops, whips, and walking sticks on it. I remember thinking: *Fuck me, this is a serious dom place,* when I first saw this room. But hey, I wasn't there to judge, I was solely there to earn money.

I remember the two girls who I had working for me on my first shift at *BJ's*. They were called Sarah and Megan; both lovely people who made my first day easy and smooth. Sarah was a curvy, busty blonde, who was quite pretty. She was probably in her late thirties back then. Megan was a petite brunette with small boobs, who was about the same age as Sarah. I found them both easy to sell when I was speaking to customers on the phone, as they were the complete opposite to each other. I'd advertise them as Ebony and Ivory (brunette and blonde).

Nicola Harper

Wacky Wednesdays

The first day I worked at *BJ's* was a Wednesday and BJ would hold her own Wacky Wednesday session with clients that she'd had for years. I'd never experienced anything like this before. I have to admit that the first one I saw gave me quite a shock. It started at around 1 pm. Sarah and Megan had both been busy all morning and the parlour had finally fallen quiet for a bit. The girls were both sitting with me in the small reception area, eating their lunches. The buzzer went off and I looked on the CCTV and saw that an elderly gentleman with a well-groomed beard was standing outside. I released the buzzer and let him in. He walked up the stairs and as he came through the door at the top, both Megan and Sarah looked over at him.

"Hi Lesley," they said.

"Hi girls," he replied. "Where's BJ?"

"In the kitchen," Sarah said.

"Thanks," Lesley said, as he walked off in the direction of the kitchen. At this point, I didn't think anything of the situation. I just presumed that Lesley must be a friend of BJ's. I didn't think he was a customer, he knew exactly where the kitchen was, and I thought he must just pop in to see his friend from time to time.

Then the buzzer went off again. Another, even older, gentleman appeared on the camera. I buzzed him in and he walked up the stairs. As he came through the door, he looked at me and said:

"You must be the new receptionist."

"Hi, yes," I said. "I'm Nicole."

"I'm Norman," he said. "Is BJ in?"

I told him that she was in the kitchen, so off he went, just like the first older guy. After that, another five men came in looking for BJ, and I told them all that she was in the kitchen. Each of them headed straight there.

About thirty minutes later, BJ came out of the kitchen. "Come on, ladies," she shouted.

Behind her came one of the strangest processions of people that I've ever seen. BJ was at the front - dressed from head to toe in PVC, and she was holding a dog lead. Attached to this lead – naked and on all fours – was one of the men who I'd buzzed in. He was crawling as fast as he could to keep up with her, so that she wouldn't choke him when she pulled the lead. Lesley, the first older chap who came in, was now dressed in black stockings, a black frock and black panties. He had silver nipple clamps attached to his extremely long nipples. BJ was screaming at him:

"Come on, Lesley Loo Loo."

Norman was following on behind Lesley. He was now completely naked, had a raging hard on, and was wearing a smug smile. There was another bloke there called Suzie Q who was dressed in drag and another who was completely dressed in PVC and wearing a gimp mask. As I stared at them, I was trying to hide the shocked expression that wanted to creep across my face. *What the fuck is going on here?* I thought.

Sarah and Megan got up and followed BJ and her wacky customers into a room. What happened for the next hour was quite different from anything I'd ever witnessed before. BJ sat down on the bed, screaming at all the men. She had Lesley licking her PVC boots. Norman was getting sucked off by Suzie Q the transvestite. Sarah was spanking the guy on the dog lead really hard with a riding crop. Megan was feeding poppers to the man wearing the gimp mask (i.e. making him sniff it) and BJ was just sitting there on the bed like the Queen of Sheba all the while, telling all the guys what to do to each other. They all did exactly what she asked and each time they replied to her they said: "Thank you, Mistress."

One of the men chose to stay in the corner of the room on his own, masturbating. BJ's eyes soon clocked him. "Martini Man, what are you doing?" she yelled. "Masturbating, Mistress," he replied. Apparently, he was called the Martini Man because he was up for anything, anytime, any place, anywhere, like in the 1980's advert.

"I didn't say you could masturbate yet, did I?" BJ screamed at him.

"No, Mistress," he replied.

"Come here," she yelled at him.

Martini Man walked towards her very slowly, a smirk on his face. BJ bent over the side of the bed and picked up a huge black, rubber dildo – which was probably the size of a baseball bat.

"Bend over," she shouted.

The Martini Man did just that. Then he pulled his butt cheeks apart. BJ pushed this enormous dildo right up his arse.

"Sit on that," she screamed.

"Yes Mistress," Martini Man replied, clenching his butt cheeks together so that the dildo remained up his arse while he sat on the floor with it still up his bum.

During the next half an hour, anything went in that room. Guys were sucking each other off, Megan was spanking the gimp guy, BJ and Sarah were pissing on the guys on the floor. It was basically a dom orgy. At the end of the session, everyone got dressed and things went back to normal. I noticed how the atmosphere and conversation immediately changed, as soon as people had their regular clothes on.

"So what are you up to for the rest of the day, Lesley?" BJ said. "I'm going shopping now," he replied. "My wife thinks I've gone to Morrisons, so I've got to go and get the food for her before I go home."

How bizarre, I remember thinking. *You've just sucked five other blokes off and your wife thinks you're in a supermarket.* Just goes to show how some people live.

Nicola Harper

Success in Selling

I liked *BJ's* from the moment that I started working there and I loved the weird and wonderful customers who would come in. It was so different from an office environment – where every day of your life is pretty much the same. In the sex industry, no two days at work are ever alike. All of *BJ's* customers were unique, and had the most interesting requests.

When I stared working for BJ, she saw how many more customers I could pull in than she was used to. To start with, she had two rooms and two girls working in them. To be honest, I've always been able to sell. And working on the desk in a parlour is no different to selling broadband. If you know your product, you can sell it, it's as simple as that. You just have to study whatever product you want to offer and then elaborate on it, basically. Even if it's a woman. You just exaggerate what you're selling. I'm good on the phone and I can adapt to different people. So, if a customer who was posh phoned up, I would put on the airs and graces, and, if it was a bit of rough, I'd have some banter with them. I'd just adjust to whoever I was talking to. And BJ liked this, she saw that I was good at what I was doing.

So, initially, there were two girls and two rooms at BJ's. But she had three rooms; there was a dungeon in the middle of the other two. And I was losing customers, because two girls can only do so much in a day. The dungeon was a wasted space. So I told BJ that we should put another bed in the middle room, and get a third girl to come in and work. BJ thought about this for a bit, then told me she'd try my idea for a month and see how it all worked out. So before long, we'd got three rooms, three girls, and were open seven days a week.

But I found that I was still losing customers. Three girls just couldn't cope with the amount of customers that I was able to pull in on the phone. I then told BJ that I needed a fourth girl, so then I was juggling four girls and three rooms. Shortly after that, BJ decided to move the space inside the brothel around and convert it. So we split one of the massive rooms in half, so now we had four rooms and the same number of girls. And then the numbers of punters coming in started going through the roof, which was brilliant. BJ went from having an income of fifteen to twenty customers per day, to having fifty plus customers coming in each day.

One day, from ten in the morning until eight at night, I was able to pull eighty customers in. It's a lot, that. If you've got the gift of the gab and you can sell, then this kind of thing works. I would do things like put two guys in with one girl at once, if the girl was happy with that. Immediately, you've got a double payment for one girl and one time slot. Or, I would put three men in with one girl, because then they would all interact with each other. And the money then comes rolling in. Simple.

Perhaps because this parlour was so different from *The Edwardian* and *The Pelican*, it attracted a different clientele. We had customers turn up from all parts of the country, looking forward to having their deepest, darkest desires met. A lot were curious; they would come in to try things that they'd always fantasised about but had never done. Lots of trannies came in, I'd never dealt with so many before I started working at *BJ's*. Lesley Loo Loo was one of them; the guy who'd come to *BJ's* Wacky Wednesday session. When he was at home, he had a wife who was an air hostess, he worked in an office, he was very respectable and well spoken, and had a normal life. He looked a bit like Sean Connery. But when he came in to *BJ's*, he'd be wearing nipple clamps, a Basque and stockings, and he would say things like:

"Please can I get changed, Miss?"

And I would have to say: "Yes, off you go."

I still see Lesley Loo Loo every now and again. There was also a guy called Suzie Q – also a Wacky Wednesday regular. In the outside world, he was a normal man who worked in a factory. He came across as very masculine. But when he came to *BJ's* he'd be wearing stockings, suspenders and a Basque. Whereas Lesley Loo Loo would like to come in and do the cleaning and be told what to do, Suzie Q would prefer to walk around with nipple clamps on while sniffing poppers. Suzie Q loved cock. He couldn't get enough of it. Honestly, the customers in BJ's were all next level. While I'd had freaky punters prior to working there, the men who came into my new place of work were just different. Much weirder, on the whole.

BEHIND THE BUZZER

The Girls & 'Girls' at BJ's

I absolutely loved working at BJ's when we'd got the business properly up and running. It was fun, with it being so busy. We were both making loads of money and everybody was happy. The girls who worked there were smashing it and eventually, I had a tranny on every day as that's what the customers wanted. The tranny – Danielle – was stunning; he was a young gay lad, only twenty one, and he just looked beautiful when he was all done up. With a blonde wig and make up, he was prettier than any of the girls. Men would come into the parlour, point at Danielle, and say: "I'll have her." So I'd have to take the guy somewhere private and tell them that he was a tranny, because you couldn't tell just by looking at him.

I liked Danielle. She was a right diva and, in some ways, she was harder to work with than the girls, what with her bitch fits. But she was a great person, financially motivated, and always very busy. It's crazy, because when I look back and see how many straight married men would travel for miles to see our transvestite Danielle, I can't believe it. But then, maybe gender and sexual orientation is a lot more fluid than society thinks. I can't count the number of times a 'straight' guy would pretend he didn't know that Danielle was a transvestite and then go along with the service anyway when I told him. What I've found with bi-curious guys over the years, is that if they have the illusion that it is a woman with a man's penis who is servicing them, they find it easier to deal with. Maybe they can convince themselves that they are still having sex with a female? Who knows.

Eventually, we had another tranny on – Mel – who was actually Graham the Dog who I'd serviced when I worked at *The Pelican*, the one who liked to wear a gimp mask and be fed dog food. By the time I'd got *BJ's* up and running, Graham the Dog had undergone a massive transformation, and had become Mel the tranny. He never talked about the Dog days, because he seemed disgusted by how he'd behaved back then. I never did find out exactly what caused him to change like this, but people do sometimes, don't they? When he was Mel, he acted like a posh woman. Bit weird, but there you go.

The girls at BJ's were all nice; there was one called Amber who was more mature, very pretty, with long blonde hair and piercing green eyes. She was a friend of BJ's and had worked there for years. There was also Sarah, a chubby girl who I got on well with. Then there were Celeste, Claire, and quite a few more. I used to throw orgies on a Sunday and all the girls and guys would pile into one room, because it was easier. The guys all had a service and everyone was in and out in half an hour. And they were all happy and interacting with each other. That was the Sunday pile-in.

Now, I did come across one girl in BJ's that turned out to be an illegal immigrant. But I genuinely didn't know she was, until the very end when she had to leave. It was quite a sad state of affairs. She was a Chinese girl – I gave her the working name Tiger Lily – and I asked her to bring me her passport just so she could show me that she had the right to live and work in the UK. So she brought her passport in, I took photocopies of it, and that was that as far as I was concerned. In the end, Tiger Lily and I got really close. This might have been partly due to the fact that the other girls didn't really talk to her; perhaps because she was from another country, I don't know. One day, Tiger Lily opened up to me and told me how it was that she'd come to work in England. Basically, she said that she was trafficked over and that a triad was in charge of her.

They told her that it was her duty to work for them in different Chinese parlours all over the country and they said that when she'd grafted eighteen thousand pounds for them, they would let her go; she would be free to leave them and do whatever she wanted. So she did her time with this triad, earned them eighteen grand; then they gave her a passport and she was free to go and live her life in England. Tiger Lily said that Thai girls have to earn the triads even more than the Chinese ones before they are set free. It's so awful, how they're treated. Anyway, after she was freed, Tiger got a job working as a prostitute at *BJ's*, and that's how I got to know her. I developed a bit of a soft spot for her as she was so nice. When I was pregnant, she gave me a teddy for the baby, which I still have at home today.

But then one day, one of the girls who worked at *BJ's* – who was a complete bitch called Janine – decided to try and get Tiger Lily to agree to having an arranged marriage with her brother. She wanted Tiger Lily to pay her twenty thousand pound for this privilege. I warned Tiger about this, and told her that the girl was trying to rip her off. I thought that she'd been through enough shit already and that she didn't deserve to have this girl fuck her over like this. The bitchy girl – Janine's - plan backfired, Tiger didn't go through with this arranged marriage and then Janine got pissed off because, by then, I'd sacked her because she was so unpleasant and aggressive. She would always drink too much and then turn on people. BJ was too scared to sack Janine herself, so I did it. As a result of all this, Janine turned on Tiger – perhaps she blamed her in some way? – and she rang the police and told them that Tiger Lily was an illegal immigrant who shouldn't be working in the UK. So one day, when Tiger was working a shift, the police turned up together with the immigration people. I got the copies of her passport out of the cupboard and showed them to anyone who wanted to see, but the immigration people checked her details on their computer and said that the passport was false, illegal. So they arrested the poor girl. They took her to the police station and booked her, and then let her go and told her to come back in two weeks. So obviously Tiger disappeared and the last I knew she was back in China, with plans to go and work in Australia.

I've worked with European girls before and because I see how they are behind the scenes, I won't have them working for me in my current parlour. As a customer, you don't see what goes on in that back room, you just see the girl coming out to reception in her underwear with a fantastic figure, looking very young and smiley. But what you don't see is the very same girl in the back room on the phone to her boyfriend, crying her eyes out because she's really worried that she hasn't made enough money for him that day. All that the pimps of those European girls allowed them to bring to work were ten cigarettes, some home-made butties, and two cans of energy drink. This pitiful amount was supposed to keep them going for hours, even though prostitution is a really physically demanding job.

Once these girls had done one shift at a parlour, their pimp might take them straight to another one and expect them to do another full shift. They are treated so badly, it's unreal. It's for this reason that I refuse to employ EU girls. I don't agree with how they're treated at all. They have no control over their lives. Their pimp boyfriends take all their money and send it back to whatever country they're from, and they'll buy land and build these huge fuck-off type mansions on it. But they didn't earn the cash that they're spending, the poor girls working for them did. And that's what goes on. And it's why I won't have them working in my brothel. I won't have it, it's as simple as that.

Madam BJ

BJ was not what you'd expect at all in a madam. She wasn't the typical boss of a brothel. She'd previously worked as a prostitute herself, was tiny in height – about four foot nine inches tall – had red hair and a broad Mancunian accent. She wasn't up her own arse like some madams can be, in fact she was quite shy and down to earth. But – as with most people – there was another side to her. If you crossed her, then you'd know about it. Luckily, I always got on well with her.

BJ was noticeably different from Ethel and Vera, my previous bosses. She was just more earthy, with her broad Manc accent. Whereas the others had more airs and graces, BJ would wear tracksuits – not the posh velour ones Vera wore – and was just Wythenshawe in her attitude. We got on well and I was making BJ good money, so everything was ticking along nicely at that stage. We'd go to each other's houses sometimes and BJ would buy my daughter little things. Looking back, these were more like rewards, as I was making her so much money.

BJ left it up to me to manage everything, which I was happy with. I did the hiring, the firing, the rotas, the stock, everything. BJ wouldn't have to worry about anything; she'd just come and collect her envelopes with her money in and then go. The girls were good, they weren't addicts or anything, so it was a happy ship and everything ran like clockwork – for several years at least.

Chapter Fifteen
Role Play

To be honest, we got a lot of freaky customers at *BJ's*. People knew that if they had a particular fetish, then they could come and feel safe indulging in whatever they were into at that parlour. It was one of the wackiest places I've ever worked in. Anybody was welcome and they knew that once they'd walked through that front door, they could have their wildest fantasies fulfilled.

Wubber Man

Sarah – one of the girls who I worked with – was one of my favourites. She would always be happy when she came in to do her job and never moan about any of the customers. She would just get on with it, make her money, then go home. I like people like that. Sarah was very good at her job and her acting skills were fantastic. She was always very popular with the customers. I remember that there was a little old man who would often come in and see her. She called him the 'Rubber Man'. He spoke with a very strong lisp, so every time he said the word 'rubber' it would sound like 'wubber'.

Rubber Man was probably in his sixties back then. He would arrive at BJ's very well dressed, in a smarty suit, shirt, tie and shiny brown shoes. He always carried a bag with him. Like I've mentioned before, as soon as you see a customer with a bag, you know something freaky is about to happen. Rubber Man would only ever book Sarah, as he felt so comfortable acting out his fantasies with her. She would take him into the room and he would strip off his clothes until he was completely naked. He would then put on a pair of wellies and get Sarah to wear another pair. After that, they would both put on a pair of rubber Marigold gloves. Then Rubber Man and Sarah would lie on the bed together and he would stroke her with his Marigolds, saying:

"Ooh Sarah, smell the wubber!"

Sarah would have to pretend that she was getting off on this rubbery smell. She would say to the Rubber Man:

"Ooh, the smell of rubber makes me so horny, it's making my pussy wet."

The Rubber Man loved to hear her saying this and fully believed that she was getting wet from the smell. Towards the end of the service, Sarah would have to put one of her hands near his nose so that the smell of her rubber glove was very strong for him. At the same time, she would have to masturbate him with her other hand, that was still wearing the other glove. Rubber Man would squeal with delight:

"Ooh Sarah, smell the wubber. The wubber is turning me on!"

Eventually, he would spunk all over Sarah's Marigold, then wipe himself down, get dressed and go home. I quite liked this guy. He was a good regular, knew what he wanted, and was no bother at all.

Kenneth & his dalliance with death

Another customer that stands out is Kenneth the lorry driver, who used to come into BJ's quite often. In fact, he still comes into the parlour I own today; we've known each other for years now. He's another one who brings a bag with him and as soon as they see it, the girls know that Kenneth wants to get freaky. In his bag, he has duct tape, black bin bags, cling film, poppers, industrial masks, tights, and a few other weird things.

Whoever takes Kenneth into a room soon finds out that it takes ages to get him ready. He likes to be wrapped from head to toe in black bin bags and cling film, with just a hole left for his nose so that he can sniff his poppers. Also, so that he can breathe. There has to be another hole for his tiny penis to poke through. The first time anyone sees him all wrapped up like this, they can find it a bit daunting. But everyone soon gets used to him. Once the preparation is all done and he's wrapped from head to toe, you have to drug him up with the poppers; he likes to have two bottles stuck together – one for each nostril – so that he gets absolutely off his head. Then all the lights are turned off in the room.

Then someone has to start whispering in his ear, telling him that he is going to be buried alive, that his wife is never going to see him again, that she doesn't give a shit about him anyway, that he is going to be taken into the woods and all the maggots and worms there are going to eat him, and he's going to die. As you're saying all this to him, you have to wank him off and you also have to say to him that his sperm is going to be used for scientific research. Then you can go out of the room and leave Kenneth in there for hours by himself. He likes to be lying on his back for all this, although sometimes he has it done while he's sitting in a chair. This whole routine really turns him on. You just have to get into his head with the whispering.

Well, one day in *BJ's,* a girl called Celeste had gone into a room with Kenneth. She tied him up with the black bin bags and cling film, laid him down, gave him the poppers, and all of a sudden there was a massive croak. It turned out that he'd done too much poppers and as he was lying down he'd passed out and his head had crashed straight through the stud wall of the room. I couldn't get through the door, because his body – all wrapped up – was a dead weight. Eventually, I got through to see him and we managed to revive him.

On another occasion, I'd had an idea for some fantastic role play that I thought would really play into Kenneth's weird fetishes. But unfortunately, it kind of backfired! He'd brought a crucifix in with him, and nailed it to the floor. This was after I'd had to veto the idea of him bringing a coffin in – he'd literally begged me to allow it but I told him that there was no way a coffin would fit into one of those rooms. So, in he came with this crucifix instead. Once it was nailed to the floor, he wanted me and a girl called Amber to wrap him up with the bin bags and cling film, and attach him to the crucifix so that he was still upright. This was his big brainwave.

Now, I had this amazing idea to do something different with him. I went into the kitchen, emptied the washing up liquid bottle and put water in it. I then got my Zippo lighter out of my pocket. I walked back into the room where Kenneth was – all wrapped up and unable to see – and I opened my lighter and started wafting it under his nose, so that he could smell the petrol. Then I said:

"Amber, are you sure we're going to be all right pouring all this petrol on him, have you got the fire extinguisher ready? BJ's going to lose her shit if we set the building on fire."

As I was saying this, I was sloshing the water from the washing up bottle all over him, pretending that it was petrol. Given that Kenneth usually likes to be told that he is going to die and be eaten by maggots, I thought this was dead good role play, and that it would be right up his street. I thought he'd love the idea of being burned to death in a fire.

But as was flicking the lighter near his nose and dousing him with the water, Kenneth started going mad on the cross, wriggling around shaking back and forth. His mouth was gagged so he couldn't speak and as I watched him going nuts, I thought: *Ooh great, he's loving this.* But the strange thing was, he wouldn't let me near his dick to give him a wank. I thought: *Fucking hell, he's that excited that he can't even keep still.* So on we went, getting right into the role play, when all of a sudden Kenneth frees his head. I thought: *Something's not right here. Is he having a fit or something?* So I took the gag away from his mouth, and he shouted:

"Fucking stop! I didn't want this! I nearly died in a fucking fire once!"

At that point, he went absolutely mad. He was fuming; so angry. And after that day, Kenneth didn't come into *BJ's* for about six months, he had the right hump with me. He told me later that he actually thought that I was going to set him on fire in the building and then put him out with the fire extinguisher, and that this thought scared him half to death. So my amazing role-play brainwave turned out to be a bit of a clanger in the end.

Chapter Sixteen
More Quirky People

I've lived the life that I have for so long, that none of this shocks me any more. To me, it's normal. The fact that I see so many people living double lives – such as a happy family one with their wife and kids and a secret one as a drag queen who enjoys getting fucked up the arse by men – does give me trust issues. I'm more aware now of what goes on behind closed doors of people's secret lives that they keep separate from their loved ones. I've found that customers tend to open up to me because they know I'm not going to judge them. And I won't act like something shocks me, even if I think that what they're telling me is a bit weird. I just want them to feel comfortable and that they can tell me whatever it is that's on their mind. Not much fazes me now, I've seen that much over the years. I don't know any different, do I?

Some married guys will come in and feel that they have to justify to me why they're in a brothel. They'll say: "I do love my wife, but the thing is, she's gone off sex. I love her to death, she's my best friend, we tell each other everything, but she just doesn't want to have sex any more. So I just come in here to see you because I need sex." The thing is, some men will always need sex. And if their wife or partner has gone off it, then what are they to do? And a lot of our customers are just normal guys. I just seem to attract the more bizarre ones as well. It is what it is though, isn't it?

There was a guy we called the Naked Cleaner who used to come into *BJ's*. He went round all the different parlours. He's a bloody nightmare, to be honest. Lesley Loo Loo used to like doing the cleaning and he didn't do a bad job at it. But the Naked Cleaner just used to come in and walk round bollock naked, be an exhibitionist and say he's doing the cleaning. But I soon sussed that he was only coming in to perv off the working girls. He just wanted a shag. And he didn't even do the cleaning properly. So I couldn't be arsed with him and I don't let him come into my current parlour any more.

We had a lot of 'straight' England rugby players come in, and they were into trannies, poppers, and being shagged up the arse by a dildo or a strap on. They were butch guys and I was quite surprised by their preferences, but there you go. I can't really tell you their names as I don't want to embarrass them. I've found that a lot of rugby players are like that.

There was a posh old guy who used to come into *BJ's*, who I couldn't stand. He was snobby, he wore checked knee-high Deerhunter trousers, and he spoke like he was a member of the royal family. Very eccentric. He was so minted that you could smell the money on him as he walked through the door. When he came into the parlour, he used to book in with my friend that worked there – Diane. She does anal and all that. This guy used to bring a Tupperware tub in with him – which was obviously a sign that something strange was going to happen. He'd go in the room with Diane, put his fingers up her arse, and pick clumps of shit out of it. Then he'd put these clumps in his tub and take it home with him. He was sick, honestly. It was fucked up. Maybe he wanted to smell her shit at his leisure. Or maybe he wanted to put it in his wife's dinner, who knows. On another occasion, Diane was on her period when he came in. He put his fingers up her fanny, took her sponge out, smeared the blood all over her legs, then started licking all the clots and things off her.

This same posh guy came into my current parlour once. I remember that I had a girl called Natasha working for me at the time. He went into a room with Natasha, picked the shit out of her arse, and smeared it all over her back. I went nuts because the whole fucking room stank after that. But shit is his thing. He just loved to pick at it. Personally, I can't deal with the stuff. I go mad if someone does a shit in my parlour; I can't stand the smell.

I remember one incident that happened at *BJ's*, which ended with me throwing a man out into the street completely naked. Basically, this Asian guy had come in, and gone into a room with one of the girls. But it wasn't long before she rushed out of the room – totally hysterical. I asked her what was wrong and she told me that he had some sort of item with him, that he'd been trying to pop the condom with. So I stormed straight into the room, and took the whole room apart looking for whatever he'd been using to do this with.

The guy was going mad by now and the girl was still hysterical. She told me that he'd hidden something in the crease of his stomach, and that when she bent over and he was about to put his dick in her, he'd taken something out of his fat rolls – he was a big guy – and tried to pop the condom. Eventually we found the offending item in the corner of the room, and it turned out to be a cocktail stick. He'd been doing all this because he wanted bareback; to shag her without a condom. When I found the cocktail stick, I went absolutely nuts. I didn't let him get dressed, I immediately marched him to the door and threw him into the street bollock naked. He had to get dressed out there, with passers-by watching him.

The Martini Man – who I've talked about before, as he attended *BJ's* Wacky Wednesdays dom orgies – used to come in quite regularly. I really liked him. He was very well spoken; I think his real name was Conrad. He used to like walking around the parlour with nothing on. He was quite fat and had a big nose. Basically, he would do the cleaning, and suck lots of cocks; he'd hover around reception, waiting to see if he could get some dick. You could tell he was well educated and he was interesting to talk to. Now, there was a dildo that we kept on the reception desk and it was wider than the end of a rounders' bat. It was black and about a foot long. When we had a roomful of people waiting for their service, to help pass their time I used to put a suction thing on the bottom of this dildo, and put it on the floor, and I would get the Martini Man to squat up and down on it. It was like a party trick. Everyone would be watching this guy take this massive dildo up his arse. It was fascinating and weird at the same time. Our customers used to love this kind of thing; lots of them weren't your 'normal' types, they used to get off on watching people do things like this. It was often like a freak show in there.

Self-debasing Sissy

One of the most bizarre customers that I ever came across in my whole, entire working career was a guy who I knew as Sissy. That's the only name he ever used in the parlour, but like I've said before, punters use fake names as much as the girls do, so I've got no idea what his actual name is. I will never, ever forget the first time that I came across Sissy. It's one of those shockingly memorable moments that are hard to forget. I was at the reception at *BJ's* and was sitting behind the desk, drinking a cup of tea. The phone rang. I answered it and a man's voice asked if it was alright if he came into the brothel to do some cleaning.

"Course you can," I said. "Can I just take your name please?"

"Sissy," was the reply.

Then he said: "If I bring some maggots in, Miss, will you make me eat them?"

At that point, I began wondering if this was a wind up call. But in case it wasn't, I played along, like you do.

"No problem at all, Sissy," I said. "I'll definitely make you eat them."

As I put the phone down, I was seriously doubting whether any guy would turn up with a bag of maggots. But about an hour after I'd had that conversation, the buzzer went off, and I checked the camera. There was a man I'd never seen before standing there, waiting to come in. I released the buzzer and it wasn't long before this tall, slim, athletic-looking guy walked up the stairs and arrived in front of me in the reception area. As I gazed at him, I saw that he had dark hair, a pointy nose, was clean shaven and was dressed in blue jeans, a blue t-shirt and trainers. Also, I clocked that he was clutching a bag. *Aha!* I thought. Because the minute I saw the bag, I knew that this man wasn't going to be your average straight sex and oral kind of customer.

"Hi Hun," I said. "Would you like a drink?"

"No Miss," the man replied. His accent was broad Yorkshire. "I've come to do the cleaning. You said it would be okay when I talked to you on the phone earlier. I'm Sissy."

I took another look at him after he'd said this, thinking: *Fuck me, you've actually gone and turned up.* I'd honestly thought that the guy asking about the maggots on the phone earlier had been a hoax caller. I immediately went in to role play mode.

"Sarah," I shouted over my shoulder. "Sissy is here to do the cleaning."

Sarah walked through. I'd called her because I knew that she was fantastic at role play.

"Right, Sissy," she said. "Come through here with me, and we'll get you dressed for cleaning, there's a good girl."

Sissy followed her into one of the rooms and got changed into a pink tutu and a white bra. When she came back through (Sissy preferred being referred to as she, not he, when she was in role play mode; it was a personal choice), I handed her some Flash spray and a cloth, and she was immediately on a mission to blanch the whole building from top to bottom. I have to admit that Sissy was a fantastic cleaner, she scrubbed everywhere and never missed a corner.

Several hours later, her work was done. She came over to me.

"Can I go home now, Miss?" Sissy said.

"You may," I replied.

Sissy's face fell. "You've not made me eat my maggots yet," she said. She looked so disappointed. I stared back, making every effort not to show the shock that I felt creep on to my face. *This is freaky shit*, I thought. I cleared my throat.

"Where are they, Sissy?" I said in a stern voice. I watched as she opened her bag and pulled out a white, plastic box with a sealed lid on it. Next came a pint glass. "Here Miss," she said. "Shall I tip them into the glass?"

"Yes Sissy, and make sure you drink the lot," I shouted. I knew I had to carry on with the role play. Sissy then took the lid off and tipped loads of maggots out of the container and into the glass. *What the actual fuck?* I was thinking. *Surely this can't be happening*. But sure enough, Sissy put the glass to her lips, and swallowed the lot. She then opened her mouth to show me that all the maggots had gone down her throat, and that there were none left. I really tried hard to hide the fact that I was shocked.

"You can get dressed and go home now, Sissy," I said loudly.

"Thanks Miss," she said, and off she went into the back room to change out of her tutu and back into her normal clothes.

After that day, Sissy became a frequent transvestite cleaning slave at *BJ's*. To be honest, she never ceased to surprise me. Over the years, I've seen her drink more maggots, eat dog food, drink urine, and have glass bottles glued to her penis so she had to shatter them when she got home. She's even brought in blood worms before and asked one of the girls called Scarlett to shove them down her jap's eye. She then had the end of her penis glued shut - how she went to the toilet that day I'll never know. She would get us to write abuse on her forehead, like "Slut", "Bitch" or "Whore" – with a permanent marker – and then send her home like that.

I would often think to myself: *Why? Why on earth does she have us treat her like this?* I just didn't understand the method in Sissy's madness. So one day, while she was on all fours scrubbing the floor in her pink tutu, I said to her:

"Why do you do all these things? Are you punishing yourself for something?"

Sissy stopped what she was doing and looked up at me.

"It's my wife," she said. "She's disabled, and it's my fault."

"What do you mean?" I said, feeling shocked.

Sissy explained that when her wife had given birth to their child, it had been a very complicated delivery, and as a result her wife ended up disabled for life. How true this story is, I will never know. All the things that she did were so strange, I can't help thinking there might be more to Sissy's past than this. I think that maybe she's done something seriously wrong, that she's reprimanding herself for. She never booked in with any of the other girls for sex, she just wanted us to degrade her as much as possible. She wanted me to keep coming up with new ideas, but eventually it gets hard when you've been doing that sort of thing to a person for years.

One Sunday afternoon, when I was working on the desk, the landline phone rang. I answered it.

"Miss, it's me, Sissy," her voice said. "Can I come in?"

"Course you can, Sissy," I said.

"What do you want me to bring with me?" she asked. I racked my brains, trying to think of something different.

"A can of whipped cream and some industrial glue," I said, winging it. They were the first two things that came into my head.

So a little while later, Sissy turned up, put her pink tutu on, and started brushing the floor. I looked over at her. "Come here, Sissy," I said. "I want you to clean the shelves". I opened the doors to the cupboard where all the cleaning products were kept and noticed that for some reason someone had left a can of black Hammerite paint in it, with a paint brush next to it. *Perfect*, I thought.

"Stand here in front of me," I shouted at Sissy.

"Yes Miss," she said.

I picked up the paint and brush and painted her from head to toe in this black Hammerite paint. By the time I'd finished, she looked like a black, tribal warrior wearing a pink tutu. It was hilarious. I don't think she was happy about this latest idea of mine, but she never complained. I then demanded that she brought me the whipped cream that she'd brought into BJ's with her and also the industrial glue. We went into one of the rooms.

"Bend over the bed, Sissy," I screamed in my dominant acting voice.

"Yes Miss," she whispered, folding herself over the edge of the bed.

"Matthew, Alex, come here," I shouted over my shoulder. (They were two customers that came into the parlour quite often; I knew that they both liked to be told what to do) When they'd arrived in the room, I lifted Sissy's pink tutu up.

"Grab a butt cheek each," I said in a stern voice. They did as I'd asked and parted Sissy's bottom so that I had full access to her arsehole. I deftly inserted the whipped cream up it, by inserting the nozzle and squeezing, until the whole lot was up there. What happened next was one of the funniest things that I have ever seen occurring in a parlour. Basically, after the cream was up her I got the industrial glue to stick Sissy's arse together, as that's always what she wanted done after she'd had anything squirted up it. But what happened this time was completely different to any other. As I started gluing her butt hole shut, Sissy started moaning.

"Miss," she was saying. "It's burning."

As I assumed that this was all part of the role play, I started smacking her bottom, shouting:

"Don't be so mad Sissy, do as you're told and stop complaining."

I was in full-flow acting mode, you see. But then all of a sudden, smoke started coming out of her arse. Afterwards, we all realised that there must have been some kind of chemical reaction between the glue and the whipped cream – and perhaps the paint – and this had occurred while everything was up her bottom. Before I knew what was happening, this six foot tranny wearing a pink tutu was running round the whole building with smoke coming out her arse, screaming. By this point, I was lying on the floor crying with laughter.

Sissy arrived next to me. "Miss," she screamed. "It's burning."

Eventually the smoke stopped coming out and Sissy got changed back into her normal clothes. Off she went home, still painted black from head to toe. I didn't see her for a few months after that, but I will tell you one thing: after that day, she never ever asked me to put anything up her bottom again. I have to be honest with you, I thought that the whole incident was absolutely hilarious.

Moving On

I worked at *BJ's* for seven or eight years in total. It was sad how it ended. Basically, BJ didn't have a full driving license, but she had a car. I had one that my Dad had brought me – I'd had to stop making payments on my more expensive one after I started working on the desk, as I couldn't afford it after my income dipped. My No-claims bonus was just sitting there not doing anything. So, one day, I told BJ that I'd put her as a named driver on my insurance and then she could drive around in her car. But I stipulated that it was important for her to have a fully qualified driver in it with her at all times, because of her lack of license.

She was very happy with this and readily agreed. Everything was going along hunky dory for a while. But then one day, BJ got pulled over in her car, and told the coppers that she was me. She lied about her identity. And I ended up having to take her points. After that I walked away from BJ's. I felt betrayed by her. I'd tried to do something nice by adding her to my insurance so that she could drive her car, but when she'd got herself into a sticky situation she didn't hesitate to throw me immediately under the bus.

Also, though I'd got her business well and truly up and running, and had loads of punters coming through the door each day; once the money came rolling in, she suddenly decided to change the commission structure, which meant that my earnings would go right down. And I just thought she was a bitch for that, after everything I'd done for her. I'd literally made her thousands. And this is how she thanked me. Like the other madams, she just got greedy. There didn't seem to be any point in my working my arse off when I would no longer be getting any commission.

So I decided to leave. And what I did was to open up my own place down the road from *BJ's* and to take all the customers with me! What can I say? It is what it is.

Chapter Seventeen
Nicola, The Entrepreneur

I eventually ended up with my own parlour, *Aphrodite's*, because somebody had mentioned to me that there was a guy from Bolton called Terry who was looking for someone to run a brothel for him. This information came to me from a girl who worked in *BJ's*, Honey. Terry had initially asked her but she didn't want to do it. So she passed his enquiry on to me and, as I'd had enough of BJ by then, I was interested. BJ had hurt me too much so I wasn't about to go back to hers; I'd also had my daughter by then, so I wasn't keen to go back on my back for money. Then this deal came up at the right time, as though it was meant to be.

I discovered that Terry was a millionaire – albeit a dodgy one - and that he was willing to go fifty-fifty down the middle with the proceeds. Honey rang him and gave him my number; very soon, I was off to meet Terry in a car park in Farnworth to discuss his business idea. After we'd had a chat, Terry took me to the place that he'd bought and that he wanted to turn into a parlour. It turned out to be a big mill on a road that had terraced houses on it. I saw that the building was derelict and we went inside and up the stairs. I saw that, on the first floor, there was this massive open space. When I first clocked the enormous room, I was having doubts about whether it could be successfully turned into a brothel.

But the place was discreet, it had its own entrance – actually two, one with a car park – and Terry said he wanted to convert it all and had his own builder who was willing to do the work on it. The deal would be that he got the money back that he'd invested in it by doing it up. I thought about it and quite liked the sound of it. It wasn't going to cost me anything and I was set to get fifty percent of the income, rather than just a reception wage. I decided to go with the idea and see what happened. So I told Terry how I wanted the place to look and planned it all out. He was as good as his word and it wasn't long before all the partitions were in. Soon, we had a huge reception area with a desk and ceiling lights which was very nice. Then the first room was a dungeon and the other three were bedrooms with TV's on the walls - all en suites – and all themed. We had an Egyptian room, a Red room, a Pink room and a Blue room. The dungeon had a dog cage and a St. Andrews cross in it, along with all the accessories like nipple clamps. We decided on having uniforms for the trannies as well.

I didn't target the brothel towards any particular group of people – unlike *BJ's, that* had aimed at those with the more freaky sexual needs – but I tried to make sure that anyone who came in would have their sexual desires accommodated. I've found that if you can accept all fetishes, then it's in your interest. That way, you're catering for everything and everyone and you won't lose any business. Whereas, if you're just offering straight sex and oral, then you'll have a pretty limited market.

Even today, if people want to do something that I think is a bit peculiar, I don't show it. However, there are a few things that I will draw the line at. I don't like school girl role play, because going down that route can blur the line with paedophilia. For example, I've had it where a guy's gone in the room and asked me to pretend to be a naughty school girl, but the problem was that he wanted me to pretend to be eight years old. At that point I knew he was a nonce. Also, I can't deal with shit. I just don't like it and it makes the whole place stink. And I'm not keen on shoving things down someone's jap's eye. Other than that, most things go.

I told Terry that I'd never had a glory hole in any of the places where I worked and that I would like one in *Aphrodite's*. Basically, a glory hole is a round hole in the wall that is the right height for a man to put his dick through, so it can be sucked. We call it a blow and go. So Terry arranged for his builder to create a kind of confession booth; we ended up with two doors in the reception area; one led to one side of it and the girl went into the other and obviously there was a hole in the middle for the man's prick. We got a tattoo artist to draw a woman's face on the wall around the hole, so it looked like the hole was her open mouth. I was quite happy about that. Then we put big leather corner couches in the reception area as also stand-up sun beds and a pool table. It ended up looking really nice.

The reason I called the place *Aphrodite's*, was because the name began with an 'A'. This was deliberate on my part; I wanted a name that began with an 'A', because my reasoning was that it would then show up straight away in the alphabetical listings and be at the top whenever anyone looked up parlours. Also, Aphrodite is the goddess of love, which seemed pretty fitting. I had logos made up with Aphrodite's head on them and put them everywhere, like on the desk.

Just before we opened, I was shitting myself, if I'm honest. At that point, I'd always worked for someone else, and had never had my own place. But I realised that the success of the place lay on my shoulders and that I was starting from scratch here; everywhere else I'd worked had already been established by the time I got there and had had traffic coming through. This time it was down to me to get it up and running. But then I thought: *well, I've done the hiring, the firing, the rotas, the stock and everything for everybody else, so how hard can it be to do it for this new place? Now all I have to do is to do it for myself.* But I was scared to death, because starting your own business is a big thing. When you have people working for you, all that stress is on you and you can panic – worrying about whether they're going to make money, or whether you are going to make any. But the bonus about working with Terry was that he owned the whole building, so I didn't have to pay any rent or bills, and he just wanted back the money that he'd already ploughed into it, plus fifty percent of the income. Which was fair enough.

I took a girl called Kerry with me from *BJ's*, and the tranny Danielle, but most of the people who came to work for me were friends that I'd grown up with and my cousin Gina. The strange thing was that, although I'd built *BJ's* up and believed that I had a better relationship with the girls there than BJ did, when push came to shove, most of them stayed back, working for her. That really hurt me. But I knew that as soon as I left, because the authority, rules and regulations would be gone, *BJ's* business would dip. And I was right, it did.

I advertised my new place by putting it in the Sunday Sport newspaper, because that was how you advertised back then. Nowadays, of course, it's all online. And I got customers who I knew used a forum where punters go, to put an ad on there as well. And, as a result, *Aphrodite's* was busy from day one. Luckily, customers from *BJ's* followed me when I opened the new place too. It was really good in there, it was a nice atmosphere, and I even had people coming in just to use the sunbeds. We held sex parties in there and the whole thing started ticking along very nicely indeed. My cousin Gina was at the reception, she was ripping me off from the start but I didn't realise that until much later on. It turned out that she was doing glory holes without my knowledge, then not recording this on the books and taking all the money. I should hate her, given everything she went on to do with me with my husband Graham – which we will come to much later on. But I don't. She's in a sad state now, a smack addict who's started injecting. She's got five kids – grown up now – and she's spending all their money on drugs. It's such a shame. Things can go downhill quite fast once an addict starts digging – injecting – especially if they're greedy with it. But there we go, what can you do?

Before I opened up this brothel, I did something quite funny. As you drive into the cul-de-sac where it was, there was a row of five houses. What I did – to ease neighbourhood relations – was to knock on every single door, introduced myself, told them what the business would be about, and invited them all in for tea, coffee and biscuits! My idea behind this was that I needed to keep the neighbours on my side as it was a residential area. So I had a meeting for them in the parlour, with lots of snack and drinks, and some of them were making comments like:

"Ooh, I've never been in a brothel before."

"Ah, it's not like what I thought it would be."

"I wonder why there's a round hole in the wall over there?"

So, basically, all the neighbours came in for a nosy round, which kept them sweet. One of them, Alison, was a big fat lady with blonde hair who lived on her own. She was probably in her late fifties back then. She owned a Staffordshire bull terrier, but, apart from him, I don't think she had much of a life. From the offset, after my friendly neighbourhood meeting, Alison would come into my parlour every day for a chat, and end up staying all day till we closed. We all got matey with her and she would sit and chat with the customers. I just seem to attract those sorts of people, if I'm honest: the waifs and strays of society who need somewhere to belong. The type who you give a bit of attention to and suddenly they think they're your new best friend. But I liked Alison and I didn't really mind that she came into *Aphrodite's* so much.

Now, I'd had a webcam installed in one of the rooms, so when the girls weren't doing customers, they could go on the webcam and keep earning money (although I'd blocked out the UK). I put loads of sex toys in that room and my plan was that if the police ever came sniffing around we would just say we were doing camming – which is legal. Anyway, this Alison ended up going on the cam, getting her tits out and talking sexy to all the people abroad who were watching. She really came out of her shell after she started coming into my parlour – she absolutely loved it in there. When I got raided and had to close, she was gutted, as it had become her life.

We had a right laugh in *Aphrodite's*. Like I say, the atmosphere was brilliant and we were always busy. Just before we opened on the first day, I was dreading it – in case no one turned up. But it all went really well. We had three girls on that day and they did twenty eight customers between them, which isn't bad at all. The customers who were coming in were a mixture of *BJ's* old ones who had followed me and new ones who had seen the ads I'd put about. People liked it in *Aphrodite's* because it was a bit more upmarket than *BJ's* – not as shabby –, it had been done nicely inside and was kitted out with a pool table and loads of other things. We didn't have a bar, but what with the sunbeds and the glory hole, the customers were kept busy when they were waiting in reception. I found it useful to learn from other people's mistakes and after working in the three other parlours previously, I had a good idea of what would work and what wouldn't.

The whole place soon smelt of sex and poppers. I held a lot of orgies in there, so the naked bodies would add to the general aroma. I also remember it smelling of wood, because we'd had a brand new laminate floor fitted in the huge reception area. There was also a tinge of a damp scent in the building and I remember how cold it could get in there, because the building was huge – a mill – that had undergone a conversion. Even though it looked modern inside by then, the smell of 'old mill' still always lingered in the air. The constant sound of moans and groans would fill any visitor's ears when they came in, as men were always getting sucked off in the glory hole – just off the reception area. You could always hear when a bloke was about to come, because the stud walls were quite thin. You could also hear the clapping noise coming through the walls when one of the girls was being pounded in a room by one of the customers and his balls were bashing on the girl's ass.

There was a guy, Mark, who came in during the first week. He liked to wear thigh high PVC boots and be fed poppers. Kenneth came in and so did Horseman Harry. Now, Harry was really intrigued by the glory hole – they all were. It was something new. It wasn't long before he decided to go into it and he wanted me to do his service. But, obviously, I didn't do that sort of thing any more – not since my daughter's Dad had said he was uncomfortable with me working as a prostitute even while I was still at *The Pelican*. So I devised a plan.

I said: "Yes of course I'll do it, Harry."

So off Horseman Harry went into his side, but of course he couldn't see who was round in the other side. It was a confession booth basically, you just couldn't see who was in the other compartment. There was no light in there, so everything was pitch black; the bloke couldn't see who was giving him the service. Once Harry was in his bit with the door shut, I beckoned the Martini Man to come over, because I knew he liked sucking cock.

"Go in there and suck his dick," I whispered to him, pointing at the other compartment. So off he went – happy as Larry - and started sucking Harry's cock. Now Horseman Harry soon realised that it wasn't me, but he carried on with the whole thing because he secretly liked a tranny sucking his dick, even though he pretended he didn't.

After Horseman Harry had come and had cleaned himself up, I saw him leaving the booth, so I wiped my mouth and said: "Ooh, that was good that, Harry." He looked at me with a smile on his face, shaking his head. "I know your fucking tricks, Nicole," he said. Because he knew it was the Martini Man who'd sucked him off and not me, but hey ho. He wasn't bothered.

Aphrodite's was just so unique. People used to come in and sit there all day and treat it as a day out. They all just sat on the sofas in the reception like they were having the best of times. Not all brothels are like that, most are just run business-like; the customer comes in, gets his service, pays and goes. But all of mine have always had more of a community spirit and I like that. It suits me down to the ground. As long as the customers are booking in and paying their way, I'm not bothered about how long they stay. It turns into a social day out for them. Even now, in my current parlour, I often end up ordering dinner for anyone who's around during dinner time, some even stay for two meals. The way I see it is that if you keep the punters sweet then they'll come in during most shifts and it's good for my business. And they stay loyal to me. You just have to respect the fact that they're spending money on your premises and adding funds to your pot each week.

It's nice, because the customers have a sense of belonging in my parlours and they all get to know each other. They'll sit there discussing the football together or sharing information about the girls who work there. It's like they're having a group meeting about all different things. Also, they're all on first name terms with each other. It's like a social club. And I like that, because it works for me; it's financially viable for me to have it like that and when I'm at work, I like to have people around me. When I'm at home I'm the total opposite; I like to be on my own so that I can recharge my batteries.

Now, the guy from Bolton – Terry – who'd bought the mill and who I'd gone into business with over *Aphrodite's*, was never a customer there, but I did end up having a relationship with him. But as he already had a partner, there was no way that our affair would have worked long term. I was his bit on the side and he kept telling me that he wasn't with this other woman, but the reality was that he was. In the end, he told me that he just couldn't get rid of her because she was getting over cancer, and he couldn't upset her like that when she was so vulnerable. In the end, Terry turned out to be a twat, if I'm honest.

He could see that I was financially viable for him, especially after I had the brothel up and running and it was so successful. He could quite easily see what he was getting out of me. But I had issues with him much later on, when he lent me some money to open another parlour, but we'll come to that much later down the line. I ended up seeing Terry on and off for quite a while, but he went back on his word over something, so we fell out. But like I say, we'll get deeper into that at a later point.

Aphrodite's was going really well; we had a lot of sex parties where people would shag on the pool table and the corner couches. One of the girls was fucking a dentist outside work and word got around that he did veneers. So the girls who worked for me started a kitty between themselves and they all saved up and had their teeth done by this dentist! I helped them save, they would each give me fifty pound a shift or something, and eventually they all had enough to get their veneers done with this guy. I didn't get mine done with him, I got mine done a few years later with someone else.

Rob, the Splosher

One guy who sticks in my head – who came into that parlour – was called Rob. I'd never seen him before the day that he came in and I've never seen him since, thank God. He was originally from Scotland and was probably in his twenties at the time. He was short in height, had dark hair, and was plainly dressed. He rang up one day and asked if we did sploshing. Now, I didn't know what the bleeding hell sploshing was, but I said "Yeah, no problem". My reasoning was that we did pretty much anything at *Aphrodite's*, so it didn't matter too much what he actually wanted to do.

So a little while later – when I was at the reception - this Rob came clunking up the stairs holding all these big bags. He had a camera, buckets and all sorts with him. He looked at me and said: "I'm going to be in here for a while, but I will pay well." "Okay," I replied, wondering what was about to go on.

He picked a girl called Sienna to be part of whatever it was that he was planning. And then he started to get everything ready. As I was watching him blowing up a paddling pool, I was thinking: *Right, what the fuck is going to go on here then?* This was all happening in the reception area. Then he set up a tripod and placed a video camera on top of it. And then he started getting all these buckets ready. He took them into the bathroom, put flour in each one of them, and mixed water with it – stirring it round and round – until the mixture had a thick texture. Rob then squirted grey poster paint into each bucket and mixed that in. I began to realise that he wanted this concoction to look like it was cement.

After this, Rob had us all sitting in the reception area and he asked me to put a DVD that he'd brought with him on the big screened TV we had in there. So I did what he asked, and we all proceeded to spend the next forty minutes watching the most boring film in the world, which was about diggers and cement mixers. We were all bored out of our minds but this Rob was totally mesmerised by the diggers. He told me that he was autistic and before he said that I was already wondering about him, because there was no emotion in his eyes. His face was like blank canvas and he had a dead stare. There was no light or life in him. The girls and I started looking at each other, thinking: *This is bloody weird. What the fuck's he doing here?*

Thereafter, Rob put these step ladders by the paddling pool and told Sienna to get completely naked and stand in the pool. The camera was set dead precisely, trained exactly on to Sienna – it had taken him all day to get this right. He directed Sienna how to stand, telling her to move her arm a bit and things, until everything was to his satisfaction. He was dead meticulous about everything. Then, once he was happy with everything, he brought a filled bucket, climbed up a step ladder, and poured the grey cement-like mixture on top of Sienna's head. She had to pretend that she was drowning in cement, that she was dying. He had her saying things like:

"Help me, oh I can't breathe."

He wanted her to really exaggerate how awful it was for her. At the time, it was funny; poor Sienna had to spend all of the next day getting clumps of dyed grey self-raising flour out of her hair. But looking back, the whole of Rob's set up seems very strange indeed. There was something very dark about what he was doing; the silence that he liked us to sit in that day, the boring film about diggers, the complete lack of emotion in his eyes, the fact that he was so meticulous about everything, the positioning, the camera, and the fact that he wanted Sienna to pretend that she was drowning in cement – dying in such an awful way.

It was like he was practising for something, or re-living something he'd already done. If you started speaking while the DVD was playing, he would tell you to shut up and watch it. It was like he had no feelings at all. Rob was really, really freaky, he wasn't right. And I was glad that he never came back to *Aphrodite's* after that. Maybe he's buried people alive in cement before? His dead eyes were the scariest thing about him.

There was another guy who used to come into *Aphrodite's* called Martin. He was a freak who went round all the parlours. He used to book with a particular girl each time he came in and ask her for 'fart fetish'. What he would do, was to go into the room with her for half an hour; she would have to kneel on the bed on all fours and, then, would basically have to fart in his mouth as much as she could. If the girl couldn't perform, then he wouldn't tip her. Weird, eh?

One day, a racing driver called Graham came in; he worked with cars for years, but then one day had been involved in a crash, and had had to have his face partially reconstructed. Now, Graham was partial to drink. His routine was to come in and have a bottle of wine at the reception. I thought this was mad behaviour personally, because he'd already been horrifically injured in a crash once, yet he would come to mine, get pissed, then drive himself home. I don't agree with that kind of thing at all, to be fair. On the particular day that I'm thinking of, Graham had worked his way through several bottles of wine. Mike was there too, the guy who used to be Ethel's – from *The Edwardian's* - minder. He'd been best friends with Ethel's husband, but she'd got jealous of their friendship and got rid of Mike. But I'd remained friends with him, and he was always welcome in the parlours that I ran – I still see him all the time now.

The tranny and a girl called Kenzie were working. Now, I could see that Graham and Mike – as well as Danielle the tranny and Kenzie - had really got stuck into the booze that day and were getting more and more pissed. So when they were both in a booking, and couldn't see what I was doing, I tipped all their remaining wine down the sink. I was thinking: *I can't cope with their drunkenness, it's starting to annoy me now...* Generally, I don't allow drinking in my parlours, as it inevitably leads to trouble. But as that Graham had brought the wine in with him and shared it with everyone, I'd let them get on with it, to a point. I'd been assuming that he and Mike – as also Danielle the tranny and Kenzie - were going to drink in moderation, but that ship had already sailed. All of them had been getting louder and more out of control as the evening had gone on. So there I was in the kitchen, tipping the wine down the sink, when both Graham and Mike came out of their bookings. That's when things kicked off.

We didn't really have any dramas with the staff, apart from the one that day. Danielle the tranny started shouting at Kenzie, accusing her of drinking his wine. Kenzie was screaming back, saying that, in fact, it was Danielle who had finished *her* wine. It wasn't long before they were having a full-on scrap in the reception area. Kenzie – the pretty slim girl – was punching Danielle as hard as if she was a bloke and Danielle the tranny was slapping Kenzie back as though he was a woman. At some point, Danielle's wig went flying across the room, and he started screaming bloody murder. Meanwhile, all my customers who were sat there waiting for their bookings were watching the proceedings with open mouths, absolutely gobsmacked. Mike – Ethel's former bouncer – went over and tried to get in the middle of these two. But they weren't showing any signs of calming down. His glasses ended up getting broken and then his watch got snapped in two.

Eventually, he managed to separate them and I had to take Kenzie out of the building to calm down. As we were walking down the stairs towards the front door, I was giving her a big lecture over my shoulder, explaining why we couldn't have this sort of behaviour in the parlour, and telling her why it wasn't acceptable. I was chatting away, convinced that Kenzie was behind me, listening to what I was saying. But when I got to the bottom of the staircase, I turned round, and Kenzie wasn't there! It turned out that she'd gone back upstairs and started battering the tranny again. In the end, she was so furious and out of control that we had to get Mike and all the other blokes who were there to drag her out of the building. I never saw her again after that night, which was a shame, as I'd quite liked her. I liked Danielle, but as a rule, trannies are a nightmare. When they get going, they're worse than girls; if they get half a chance, they'd cause havoc in an empty house. It took him a while to calm down and all. The whole incident was a bloody nightmare.

The Police Come A Calling

The police raid on my premises came about because of BJ. She'd seen a decrease in her earnings since I'd left and she started making calls to the police – no doubt to get me back for this – pretending that she was a neighbour who was really bothered by my brothel. It was her and that Janine, the bitchy girl who I'd fired from *BJ's*, the one who'd tried to force poor Tiger Lily into having an arranged marriage with her brother. Anyway, the police did turn up one day but they didn't realise that there were two entrances to Aphrodite's. They went up the cul-de-sac one, where Alison lived. So, we locked those gates and started only using the other entrance round the back, where the car park was.

This tactic worked for a while, but we were probably open only for about a year before the police raided again and I had to shut *Aphrodite's* down for good. BJ and Janine continued making call after call to the coppers, bitches, because they didn't want me to take the business away from their parlour. They kept pretending to be offended neighbours, who lived near my brothel. I'd gone through the bother of getting planning permission from the council and I'd told them that the business was just a massage parlour.

As it turned out, Janine actually did live very close to *Aphrodite's*, and had watched all my customers coming and going from her living room window. She never said anything to me, she just helped BJ keep phoning the police and complaining. Now, usually the police tolerate a well-run brothel, if it's not causing any problems. The reasons for this are that they know it's a safe place for the girls to work, it keeps the girls off the streets, it's a controlled atmosphere, and it's easier for the police in lots of ways, because many potential problems are prevented by the girls working in a parlour. Things like rape don't ever usually happen in good brothels because it's all supervised. So the coppers tolerate what's going on. And although they agree with what's going on, because it's not 'lawful', they can't be seen to totally agree with it.

One day, when I wasn't at *Aphrodite's*, my cousin Gina was on the desk and she rang me up.

"We're being raided," she said.

"Don't be silly," I replied, not believing a word of it.

"No, we really are," she said, and at that point I heard something in her voice that made me realise that what she was saying was true. "You've got to come over here. The police want to talk to you, Nicola."

So I left my car at my Mum's house, with my phone – as I didn't want the coppers going through that – and just took a twenty pound note with me so that I could get a taxi home after they'd questioned me. I made my way to *Aphrodite's* and saw all the riot vans parked outside it as soon as I got there. *Fucking hell,* I thought. *Here we go.* Obviously, all the residents who lived up and down the street were out, having a good look at what was going on.

So I took a deep breath and walked into my parlour and saw all these police officers milling around, wearing helmets that had cameras on the top. Some of them had sex toys in their hands, because they'd been going round collecting items out of the rooms. Suddenly, I clocked a familiar looking face over in the corner. If you remember, I'd gone to the trouble of getting planning permission from the council and the guy that I'd dealt with there was the exact one who was standing in the corner of the reception area with the police. He turned, looked at me, opened his mouth, and shouted: "Nicola! I warned you about this when I gave you planning permission." Basically, he meant that he'd warned me off running a brothel. I thought to myself: *Quick, you need to do a bit of on the spot thinking, girl. How can you manipulate this situation to your advantage?* I looked over at the council guy.

"Gary," I said. "The truth is that you propositioned me on that couch over there." I pointed to one of the corner sofas as I said this. "And I declined. And that's why we're here today, isn't it?"

All the police started smothering their smiles. Gary, the council guy, shot me a poisonous look and then stormed off out of the building. He hadn't propositioned me at all, but I knew how important it was that I diverted attention away from me and, frankly, I thought he was a tosser anyway. After that, the coppers told me to secure the building and make my way round to the police station. Two of the girls – Gina and Marilyn – decided to come with me for moral support (although really they'd just decided to come for a nosy and to see if they were going to get dragged into the mess as they'd already given a police officer their names and addresses!). So about twenty minutes later, the three of us walked into Farnworth Police Station. I remember looking at the building from the outside, before we went in, thinking how tiny and old-fashioned it looked. *It looks like something off Emmerdale Farm.*

I went inside first, followed by my cousin Gina – who, as always, had her huge tits on display and she was flicking her back combed hair, her lips smothered with bright pink lipstick. Behind her came Marilyn, who had bleached blonde hair, was covered from head to toe in tattoos, and had even more enormous boobs than Gina. It was so obvious, from the moment we walked in, that we were the girls who'd been summoned from the brothel. I remember thinking to myself, as I looked around at the sterile interior: *What the fuck is going to happen to me now?* In reality, I was scared shitless, but I was careful not to let Gina, Marilyn, or any of the police officers know that. I decided to act all blasé, like I couldn't care less about being in there.

"I've come from the Mill on Harrowby Street," to the officer behind the desk.

"The Mill?" He repeated, not sure what I was on about.

"The brothel," I whispered quietly, hoping that nobody sitting in the waiting area would hear what I was saying.

"Ah, the brothel," he said loudly, a smirk plastered all over his face.

I knew that everyone in the waiting area must have heard him say this. At that moment, I wanted the ground to open up and swallow me. Once the officer had shouted out the word "brothel", I felt that the whole world knew why I was there. Everyone around us immediately started staring at Marilyn's huge rocket launchers that were barely covered by her top. Then they looked at the three of us girls with utter disgust on their faces. We couldn't do anything but find some free chairs, then sit down and wait. The whole place was small and old-fashioned and reminded me of the one in the TV series, *Heartbeat*. All the interior walls were white and I think the floor was blue. It was really cold in the waiting area and the atmosphere was depressing. Everyone was so serious. I remember it smelling of coffee in plastic cups and there was also a slight hospital chemical type of aroma in there. The officer behind the desk had stunk of BO, so I'd been glad to walk away from him. I remember thinking that he needed to wash his pits. As I'm thinking about it, I can almost taste his BO, it was that strong.

It didn't take long before I was called through. I remember walking towards the interview room at the back of the building, thinking: *Shit, am I going to end up in jail for this?* As I was walking down the corridor towards the room, an officer stopped the one who was accompanying me, and said to him: "Can I come into the interview with you? I've never done one of these before." *Shit, this is serious*, I thought to myself. *I'm not going to get out of here. They're definitely going to lock me up.*

I walked into the room, and was immediately told to sit down. I remember there being a desk right in front of me, that had a tape recorder on top of it. There were three police officers sitting on the other side of the desk, none of them were looking friendly; in fact they all looked deadly serious. My heart was pounding and nausea was rising up my throat. I'd never been in this situation before and I just wanted to get up and run out, but I knew I couldn't. I'd get in even more trouble if I tried anything like that. It was at that moment that one of the police officers looked me straight in the eyes, leaned forwards, and turned the tape recorder on...

Postscript

What happened next will be revealed in my next book, as will the extraordinary, unexpected and heart-stopping events that unfolded in my life from that point. Guns, grenades, Charles Bronson, and a gang leader are just some of the crazy things that I will be telling you about. But they are just the tip of the iceberg, so much more unbelievable craziness will unfold; which culminated in events that nearly caused my life to end.

Chapter Eighteen
End…. not yet. What next? Just the Start

By the time you've reached this point, I imagine your head's spinning a bit. Maybe even your stomach too. You've read things in these pages that aren't easy to digest — acts of sex, degradation, cruelty, desperation, power, and pain — things most people will never see, never hear about, and wouldn't believe even if they did. Some of it might feel over the top, like a script from some messed-up film. You might be wondering, "Did this actually happen? Is she exaggerating? Is any of this even real?"

I don't blame you for asking. But let me tell you now — yes. It's all real. Every single story in here came from something I lived through, witnessed, or had to carry with me after it was done. These aren't stories made up to sell a book or stir the pot. These are my scars.

The truth is, reality can be far more disturbing than anything you'll find in fiction. People like to pretend otherwise. They want to believe the world's mostly good, that people are mostly kind, and that the darkness only exists in faraway corners or behind bars. But that's bullshit. The truth walks among us in suits and uniforms, in school runs and shopping queues, behind wedding rings and front doors. I know, because I met them. I undressed them. I listened to their secrets while they gripped me with trembling hands and called me by names their wives have never heard.

A lot of men who visited me just wanted something simple. A release. Someone to touch them, talk to them, hold them for half an hour like they mattered. But then there were the others. The broken ones. The dangerous ones. The ones who brought in their darkness like a second skin. The ones who couldn't separate pain from pleasure. And for some reason — maybe it was my face, my silence, or my refusal to flinch — they came to me in droves. Like moths to a flame. Or maybe more like rats to poison.

I didn't write this book to shock. I wrote it to tell the truth — the ugly, uncomfortable, complicated truth. And I didn't just write it for the curious reader either. I wrote it for myself. Because I needed to finally say it all out loud. To look back at everything I've kept buried and ask myself what it did to me.

The truth? I don't know who it made me.

I've been trying to figure that out. Some days, I feel strong — like I survived something no one else could've. Other days, I feel dirty, complicit, broken. I've wondered whether I helped people or hurt them. Whether I offered comfort, or just fed a sickness. Whether I was a safe place for their pain… or just a mirror for it.

That's the hardest part. I can justify my choices all day long — survival, money, circumstance, trauma. But when

I close my eyes at night, it's not the justifications that come back. It's the faces. The words. The sounds. The shame. And sometimes, the silence that followed after.

People think that women like me don't feel. That we're hardened, detached, immune to it all. But that's the biggest lie of them all. We feel everything. That's what makes it worse. I carried the weight of every man I ever let into my world. Some left quietly. Some shattered something in me that still hasn't healed. And yet, I kept going. I kept opening the door, buzzing them in, putting on the smile, playing the role.

And now I'm finally telling the story behind the buzzer.

Writing this has been like ripping off a scab that never fully closed. But it's also been a release. A way to get some of the poison out. Maybe even a way to forgive myself. I don't know if I'll ever be fully at peace with what I've done, or what's been done to me. But this book is a start.

And I'm not done. There's more to come. More stories, more truths, more doors that need to be opened. Each one has its own kind of hell behind it — but also moments of clarity, strength, and survival. I'll keep writing, because someone has to say these things. Someone has to speak for the women who are still stuck behind the buzzer, and for the ones who never made it out.

So thank you — for reading, for sticking with me, for not looking away.

www.ingramcontent.com/pod-product-compliance
Lightning Source LLC
Chambersburg PA
CBHW020409080526
44584CB00014B/1242